HOW TO HOOK A WHALE

HOW TO HOOK A WHALE

Secrets of Selling to the Ultra High Net Worth

MARCUS LIM

with PEARLIN SIOW

Marshall Cavendish
Business

Published in 2022 by Marshall Cavendish Business
An imprint of Marshall Cavendish International

A member of the
Times Publishing Group

Other Marshall Cavendish Offices:
Marshall Cavendish Corporation, 800 Westchester Ave, Suite N-641, Rye Brook,
NY 10573, USA • Marshall Cavendish International (Thailand) Co Ltd, 253 Asoke,
16th Floor, Sukhumvit 21 Road, Klongtoey Nua, Wattana, Bangkok 10110, Thailand
• Marshall Cavendish (Malaysia) Sdn Bhd, Times Subang, Lot 46, Subang Hi-Tech
Industrial Park, Batu Tiga, 40000 Shah Alam, Selangor Darul Ehsan, Malaysia

Marshall Cavendish is a registered trademark of Times Publishing Limited

National Library Board, Singapore Cataloguing-in-Publication Data
Name(s): Lim, Marcus, 1978- | Siow, Pearlin, author.
Title: How to hook a whale : secrets of selling to the ultra high net worth /
Marcus Lim with Pearlin Siow.
Description: Singapore : Marshall Cavendish Business, 2022.
Identifier(s): ISBN 978-981-5009-11-8 (hardback)
Subject(s): LCSH: Selling. | Casinos. | Rich people--Psychology.
Classification: DDC 658.85--dc23

Printed in Singapore

To my son,
Maximus Thomas Lim —

Never lose your survival instincts,
and never give up on something
that you truly believe in.

Always follow your heart.

Contents

Part Four: Execute and Close

Part Five: Moving on Up

Preface

As you are reading this introduction, one of four things must be true:

1. You are in the casino sales business and intrigued by the idea of reading what someone in the same business might have to say.

2. You are in another job in the casino sector, but aspire to be a VIP salesperson, and are thus seeking some insight into the workings of this world and what it takes to enter this niche area.

3. You have no idea what salespeople in casinos do — your best guess involves the image of a dealer, and you are interested to find out.

4. You are not in the business, but are curious about what it takes to be a good salesperson.

This is a book produced by someone who has earned a conventionally successful life. Meaning, someone who is a multi-millionaire. Someone who has climbed to the highest positions of major companies in the gaming and hospitality sector. Someone who has broken historical records for the number of billions in profit he brought in for the company. And finally, someone who spent his childhood crammed in a three-room HDB flat with seven other people.

This book is like a buffet spread, with sections heavily laden with 'delicacies' that range from distinctive and unusual memories with ultra high-net-worth customers, to what goes on in the minds of mysterious casino salespeople as they make their sale, to the toxic workplace politics that somehow exist in every industry — gaming and hospitality being no exception.

This book, strictly speaking, is not a sales book. Naturally so, because it does not aim to be one. I have no intention of becoming another faux guru, and claim this one trick will make you a millionaire. (If they truly did know such a trick, they would probably be relaxing at a multi-million-dollar mansion in the Caribbean instead of seeking guru fame.)

I wrote this book for two reasons. First, I just got fed up with salespeople that didn't know how to sell. The sheer number of bad salespeople frustrated me. Second, I fought an extremely lonely battle in my early years in this business without a mentor. The combination of toxic work culture and company politics that I was oblivious to for the longest time almost made me quit this profession, and I don't wish anyone to endure that. This is a wild shot at creating an effect bigger than myself. But regardless whether you tick all the boxes of a bullied novice salesperson or not, I have no doubt that there is something to take away for anyone who reads this book.

After all, we are perpetually selling something to some-one. Who better to learn from than someone who sold his way to success?

Introduction
Welcome to My Life

People are always blaming their circumstances for what they are. I don't believe in circumstances. The people who get on in this world are the people who get up and look for the circumstances they want, and if they can't find them, make them.

— George Bernard Shaw

That was it. In a split second, the heads of the entire Singapore sales team were laid on the guillotine. Make it into the President's Club by the end of the financial year by hitting 150% of our annual target — or die. Shamefully resign from the company, and very possibly have our names tarnished in the small and niche casino sales industry. What was explicitly on the line were our positions in the company, but in effect we had just bet the entire future of our careers in the business to the President of Crown Casino.

"What?! No, no." Where was the man who had just been announcing, with heavily put-upon confusion, how our Singapore team had "done everything" but "just couldn't get into the President's Club?" His face was ashen. For Crown casino to lose their whole Singapore sales team in one fell swoop would be disastrous. Beer in hand still, he blustered that there was no way he was accepting a bet like that and hurriedly left our table.

But it was too late. A restaurant-full of Crown staff had borne witness to my declaration. The bet was on. And damned if I wasn't going to make good on it. The only problem was —

"Why the hell," I said slowly, running a frustrated hand over my face, "did the two of you jump in on my bet?!"

I had spoken in anger over the President's snide remarks. That the other two Singapore sales team members unanimously chimed in on my bet was completely unorchestrated, and frankly terrifying. How on earth were we going to hit more than 50% of our budgeted targets with our tiny pool of gamblers in Singapore?

They exchanged a look. "I think we can do it," one of them said finally. That daring proclamation hung in the air between us, a testament to their belief that they were voluntarily putting their asses on the line alongside mine. The stakes had suddenly been raised much, much higher.

There was really only one option. "We make sure we do it." I said, the tense line of my shoulders shifting back into something sure. I banged my fist down on the table, hard. "Let's fucking do this."

And we did.

The next few months were insanity. We hustled as if our asses were on fire — and truly, the threat of being fired was very real. We were constantly organising events and tournaments of all kinds at the casino to create a purpose for customers to visit almost every other month, going after clients be they true-blue gamblers or sporadic lapse customers who enjoyed the occasional thrill, and cajoling them into coming through any means at our disposal, from persuasion to negotiation to outright pulling the favour card. It was unimaginably exhausting: day after day, month after month of keeping up such a frantic pace of non-stop hustling, a single-minded focus on nothing but *getting more customers*, subsisting on winks of sleep caught on the plane to and fro between Singapore and the Crown in Melbourne. Uncertainty and fear were the ever-present masters spurring us mercilessly on.

But what drove us even more relentlessly was our burning desire to shove the President's Club invite right back into the President's face. His little provocation turned out to be an unexpected gift that kept on giving — we were selling like there was no tomorrow and hitting truly spectacular numbers.

By year end, we had made history. We had completely surpassed our annual budgeted target. We broke all historical company records by achieving 270% — a staggeringly large percentage that was practically unheard of in an industry where other sales teams were struggling to even reach 100%.

After we thoroughly enjoyed the fully funded year-end holiday to Japan that all President's Club members were entitled to, the President came looking for me. He was talking excitedly about how Crown's number one competitor, Star casino, would be so utterly outperformed by our Singapore sales team in the coming year.

Shortly after the trip, I officially joined Star as the Senior Vice President of South Asia, with my two teammates in tow. By an unexpected turn of fate, I became Senior Executive Vice President of both North and South Asia in July of my second year — but we were billions in deficit. Three hectic months later, I brought the company back to budget. By the end of the financial year, my team broke almost all sales records known to Star. We dethroned the almighty Crown as the reigning king of the Australian casino business to seat ourselves firmly on the coveted number one place.

We achieved the highest turnover ever of 59 billion dollars. Our budget was 38 billion — we had all but exploded, going above and beyond the set target to make a whole 20 billion in pure profit. We had done absolutely, insanely ridiculous numbers. As I remember, my paycheck that year was pretty ludicrous as well.

Now, why am I telling you all this? Surely it can't just be to brag and satisfy my own engorged salesperson ego. Of course, it's a rather unsubtle attempt at assuring you of my credibility as an experienced and reasonably successful salesman — I wouldn't want to insult your intelligence by pretending otherwise. But now, I'd like you to ask yourself: Was what you just read insightful in any way? Beyond realising with a pang how shudderingly rich casinos must be, did you glean any insight into the enigmatic workings of such establishments, or the manner in which their well-trained bloodhounds sniff out profit? Hmm? No?

There's no surprise there. Usually, that's how such stories about casinos go. Most of the published literature surrounding them is decorated lavishly with glitz and glamour, a shimmering veil of secrecy that conceals any information of real value from the public's eager scrutiny. Perhaps you may be asking: how do VIP casino salespeople manage to reel in so many whales (ultra-rich individuals)? How can I become a good VIP salesperson — heck, how can I become a good salesperson at all?

Hopefully this book will end up answering most of your questions, even those about things you didn't know you didn't know. Hopefully this book will, like an exciting buffet with platters upon platters of delectable new dishes you've never seen before, open up options and possibilities previously unknown to you.

PART ONE

GAMBLING, GAMING AND WHAT I DO

1

One Odd Start

And then, as if written by the hand of a bad novelist, an incredible thing happened.
— Jonathan Stroud, *The Amulet of Samarkand*

Perhaps you've heard of brilliant entrepreneurs who just seem to have a knack for sniffing out business opportunities like a bloodhound hunting its prey. Individuals who seem to be born with the sole purpose and singular talent for making money and raking in capital at the very age you were still playing chef with Play-Doh. All you can do is shake your head in amazement, because hey, these people are just wired a different way from everyone else; they're a different breed.

But all these people have an authentic, more realistic, yet essential attribute in common that sets them apart from enough people to make them exceptional: hunger.

From my experience, a strong entrepreneurial spirit is driven by hunger. An uncontrollable biological drive to hunt and forage when the body is starving. An overpowering ambition for more. Throughout my whole life, hunger — for money, recognition, happiness — has driven me to fight tooth and nail to get to where I stand today. I believe it's the same for the majority of other successful people out there. There is no greater driving force than this pulsating mash of anger, desperation and fervent yearning.

Why is the rags-to-riches story so popular? It speaks of a hunger that most can relate to. It reassures us with the happily-ever-after we all dream will one day precede our "The End" — a small flicker of hope unfurling in our chest, an emboldening affirmation that such miracles can happen in the world. That's the whole purpose of this book, and why I want to share my own personal story: so that you can understand my journey, my highest highs and lowest lows — and when you're caught in your own low, you'll feel that flutter of hope turning into hunger, and perhaps at the end of the day, your very own happily-ever-after.

Of course, you might have also picked up this book with the single-minded purpose of seeking out concrete sales advice. Then by all means, skip my personal story. Why would anyone care about what happened to little old me, anyway? It's absolutely irrelevant to your purpose. In fact, what a nasty trick for me to pull — luring you in with promises of solid advice, only to selfishly jabber away about myself. That wasn't in the book description, you may be fuming. False marketing!

But as Otto von Bismarck rather cleverly said, "Fools learn from experience. I prefer to learn from the experience of others." Most unfortunately, I have been one such fool.

Even so, in all my folly, my experiences have acted as show-pieces in advice sessions to those who've sought them. I want to share my learnings with anyone who's willing to listen and say, please, don't make my mistakes.

A promising start

My story starts with rags and literal hunger. My earliest memory is of my parents fighting because we couldn't afford to pay the electricity bills. My father was a boat mechanic and my mother a clerk in a merchandising company. Even though I loved to eat, I refused to ask for more for fear of burdening my family. We were eight people squeezed into a single flat.

My first taste of riches came from luck: I had a "fairy godmother". How I became the godson of this lady who was a member of one of Singapore's richest families was pure, unadulterated coincidence, which she saw as divine providence. My dad was a mechanic working on her boat when he shared news of my birth and was met with visible shock: she and I shared the same birthday! She decided there and then to "adopt" me as her godson.

That one decision altered the trajectory of my childhood completely.

With a wave of her hand, she got me admitted to one of the most prestigious primary schools, Anglo-Chinese School (ACS). That was when I realised the power of immense amounts of money and strong networking which transcends the worldly rules and governmental regulations most other lowly peasants are bound by. It is worth noting that it has not been long since unfair practices backed by cheques have been made well-known, reason being that in earlier times, in my childhood era, they were simply kept unknown.

In ACS, I experienced a different kind of hunger — the kind that wells deep in your gut and hurt. My batch mates discovered that I was one of the only three students who lived in HDBs and marked me out as a "pigeon" for living in a "pigeon hole".

Relentless teasing ensued. I felt like the poorest kid in the world, watching with burning eyes as my classmates were chauffeured to school in Rolls Royces and toted their expensive comics with Rolex-laden hands.

What my first two years in this elite institution gave me was not a premium Math and English education, but ironically a sense that somehow, wealth correlated with my value as a person. Would I have been less wronged if the exclusion was due to some other reason? It may come as no surprise that amidst being bored in class, my focus landed on how to make money.

Comics being all the craze back then, I sought out the most popular comic dealer and offered my services: I'd bring him customers. Thankfully, it's hard to say no to a determined 9-year-old. In return, he let me pick out comics for free. Even as I was disappointed I hadn't been paid instead, my brain was already working a mile a minute thinking about all the possible ways I could make money off these comics.

I picked comics with the most interesting covers, and I just... kept them. In a box under my bed. Unopened — because common sense instructed me to preserve their mint condition. I soon accumulated lots of comics under my bed. My reasoning was that like all prints, comics would eventually sell out. The key was to pick out comics that would later become a hit and sell them to fanatic comic addicts for a premium.

Social radar

Here in Singapore, most of us consider entry into a school like ACS a great blessing, but it can work the other way as well. Even though we all wore the same uniform, my schoolmates had a very distinctive "radar". I was rarely befriended, because they could sense who belonged to their social class, and who didn't. Those from richer backgrounds were higher up on the pecking order, and ordered those lower down around — and those in turn sought out even poorer schoolmates to do the same to.

One of the reasons I grew up rebellious and among delinquents was because of ostracism by the better-off. I naturally sought out others who were like me.

I won't deny this is a human tendency, present among rich and poor alike. My schoolmates didn't have to be taught how to discriminate based on social class.

But among adults, those who earned their fortune behave very differently from those who inherited it. I've spent my life finding ways to learn about and work well with both.

ONE ODD START

At a time when a plate of chicken rice was 90 cents, store-bought comics ranged from 5 to 10 dollars. After sitting on a "hit" comic for eight months and waiting for it to be sold out in shops, I'd relinquish it to salivating schoolmates for easily 20 or 30 dollars. I once even sold an Issue Number 1 comic for 85 bucks — for a comic I got for free.

I started expanding my business from comics to VHS tapes. To test the upper limits of this new market, I priced each tape at an outrageous 120 dollars. Go big or go home, right? The deal was closed almost instantly. I realised that I had found a gem. No, even better, I had found a new market where demand was sky-high and I was the only supplier.

I invested in two VCR players to duplicate the tapes for 300 dollars each. The cost price of a blank VHS tape was eight dollars — I bought 50 in one go. My school bag was emptied and filled to the brim with VHS tapes. Sometimes, as I spent my afternoons looping VHS videos at a 112 dollar profit per tape, I would marvel at how not one person thought of duplicating the tapes themselves.

At 12, I was king of the world, travelling everywhere in a taxi, buying all the toys I wanted, and always having at least 50 bucks in my wallet — pretty extravagant for a primary school kid, even by the formidable ACS standards. This experience forever impressed upon me how lucrative selling to the rich can be.

That was my primary school life, bestowed by my fairy godmother. But it's certainly not to say that only me and Cinderella can get from rags to riches, abetted by some higher power. For me, what was truly powerful was my bone-deep determination that I'd do anything not to be poor again. In fact, I demonstrated this by deciding to reject the paved path to ACS secondary school that my godmother presented, instead deciding to enter a less elite neighbourhood school, to my parents' and godmother's utter incomprehension.

The Networker

It was a whole new world. For the first time, there was no need to prove that being poor didn't equal inferiority. I could connect with my schoolmates. I found a community. This happiness brought forth an overflowing exuberance I never experienced before. Perhaps that's where the extrovert in me developed and flourished, buoyed by elation and erupting with a vigorous enthusiasm so infectious my connections soon spread throughout the school, finally landing me my reputation as the Networker.

And it was through my friendships that I found new avenues of making money. My new friends were from the street, and from the street they would always procure interesting products. Having reached a certain level of closeness, they'd feel comfortable sharing with me their wares. Other friends would then ask about the very same items I was shown days before. It was a simple matter of connecting the dots. All I had to do was bridge that gap — for a hefty compensation, of course.

I continued my business of selling VHS videos — something I discovered some others were doing as well. Having found a pool of experienced suppliers, I stopped all factory work and promoted my duties to the managerial dealings of merchandising: buying and selling at a profit.

I was selling each tape at 100 dollars — a discount of 20 dollars from primary school — tapes which I would buy from my friends at five bucks. My commission fee: 95 dollars. I could even offer my customers a whole range of new, exotic titles without ever lifting a finger to scrounge or manufacture. Not having to squander time copying tapes, I had even more time to do sales.

At the tender age of 15, I appreciated the lucrative value of outsourcing. I also understood margins: it's not always about raising the price of the product. Sometimes, buying the item at cheaper rates — without it necessarily being lower in quality — could yield gratifying returns.

My dealings were so extensive that I even attained a special sort of status. The majority of the students were from some kind of triad, secret society or gang, for without "protection" of a coalition, they'd be at the mercy of all the other groups. Yet as the Networker, I was the go-between guy who was friends with everybody, and more importantly, everybody's livelihood sort of depended on me being able to survive and thrive — I was the middleman who helped sell their wares. No gang dared touch me for fear of incurring the wrath of the other gangs.

Secondary school taught me the power of network.

I went to business school for polytechnic but soon decided that I could make more as an entrepreneur than forcing my way through school. The very next day after I dropped out, I volunteered for early enlistment into National Service. Immediately after completing National Service, I got down to business.

I spent the next ten years of my life being a business-man — from starting many of my own to investing in count-less others. I made my first million before turning 21, and proceeded to make and lose a few million more over the next decade.

What we've learnt

1. Be observant of how others behave, particularly the better off. Pay special attention to how they dress and what they talk about.
2. Sales to high-net-worth customers and regular people have roughly the same approach — listening to them, understanding their needs and building a relationship, before any products come into the picture.
3. The skills you'll learn in this book don't just apply to the casino trade, but can be used to build strong relationships with high-net-worth customers in any area.

2

Casinos: Losing, Winning and So Much More

In the 1970s, Stanley Ho of Hong Kong said, "Have a casino." He had a casino in Macau. So I said, "No, over my dead body!" But the world has changed. Increasingly, people can easily fly to gambling centres just a few hours' flight away.

— Lee Kuan Yew, founding
Prime Minister of Singapore[1]

No one really knows where gambling originated, but games of chance are almost as old as human history. Sacred writings from all over the world mention it, and some even include prayers for success in the gambling halls. It was already an age-old practice by the time the Bible got to it.

Societies at large have frowned on gambling for hundreds of years, and as recently as the early twentieth century, it could land you in jail in some places. But legalised gambling came into its own in seventeenth-century Italy, when the city of Venice allowed a "controlled amount of gambling" during the Carnival season. Gambling houses came to flourish all over Europe, but the integrated experience that casinos give today owes its roots to the entertainment boom of 1950s America.[2]

Today, Las Vegas and Macau are the gambling capitals of the world, with places like Atlantic City and Melbourne opening their own casinos to attract whales and travellers alike. In fact, for a country whose leaders once actively discouraged gambling, Singapore ironically now has a hotel and casino as its most iconic building — the $4.6 billion Marina Bay Sands complex.[3]

Casinos have come a long way from being just gambling dens. Today, the same roof can house a theatre, a concert venue and world-class shopping, the grandest hotels you can find, and yes, gambling facilities. In the same building, you can spend the night, take in a show, shop your heart out, exercise and tempt fate in the gambling halls as much as you want.

For better or worse, gambling is one of the experiences people look for when they travel, and I could fill a book with the ways it's changed the world, created jobs for millions of people, and given millions more an experience they've never had anywhere else. My customers have gone from names on a list to great customers and better friends, and I'm proud to say I've had my own small part to play in that.

There's gambling, and there's gambling badly

There's an old joke that goes: "A casino is a place where you leave with a small fortune... after you enter with a large one."

Very funny. I'd like to correct the misconception that casinos are just there to run you out of your wealth. A lot of financial, credit and status loss comes not from the practice of gambling, but from gambling *badly*. No business that just drove people to bankruptcy would last very long — because no one would want to come back, and word would spread!

We *do not* gain anything by disrupting our customers' financial state. We try our best to protect them from risking and losing too much, even to the extent of tapping them on the shoulder and persuading them to leave the table after they've won (or lost) a certain amount. I've done this a number of times over the years, but it's always the customer's decision whether they want to continue. Many people, even the ultra-rich, do gamble above their means and lose everything — and it hits especially hard for the young and those with families to support.

By definition, the outcome of a game cannot be controlled or predicted. Each round is independent of the one before it; so don't be fooled by winning streaks or an almost-win. It's imperative that you take care to minimise your losses by gambling only within your means, and never gambling with money that is borrowed or budgeted for living expenses. Gambling is strictly a game of chance, not a way to get rich or solve financial problems.

Don't get me wrong. People *can* win at casinos, and win big. But government controls, such as those set up by Singapore's Casino Regulatory Authority (CRA) and others around the world, are there to protect people from their own greed and overestimated appetite for risk. The odds are often against the individual gambler, hence the expression "The house always wins". But that's where the thrill comes from — the same thrill that whale after whale gets under our roof.

The social problem is not the industry itself, but its misuse. When ordinary people gamble away their life savings, what has ruined them — the casino (which has no way of knowing their entire financial situation or predicting their gambling habits in advance), or their gambling with money they couldn't afford to spend?

One of the reasons why we reach out to high-rollers, instead of average folk, is that they can absorb more risk without impacting other areas of their lives. That's not being unfair or underhanded — it's just the way things work.

The bottom line: Just as drunk drivers are misusing their cars, gamblers who consistently lose money are misusing casinos by not deciding in advance how much they are going to bet, how much they are prepared to risk, and how much is enough to retire for the day. And just as we keep children out of the driver's seat until they're old enough, we need to help manage the customer experience so they don't bet too much before they're ready.

However, given the crowds who come to try their luck at the slot machines, the roulette wheels and the baccarat tables, there's simply no way we can hover over everyone. As marketers and hosts, we're responsible for the experiences of our customers — so there's no mother hen for the average person who just wants to try their luck.

Two foreign-owned casinos set up shop in Singapore in the 2000s, and as I write, the government is managing the social consequences. When ordinary people like you or me visit, in place of a handler there are various protective measures in place, such as:

- A day account, where customers put in how much they can afford to risk for that day's gambling. All bets are drawn from that account, and when they lose all of it, they are not allowed to re-enter the casino for 24 hours.

- A self-exclusion order, where people have their own (or family members') identities noted for prohibition from entering any casino in Singapore.

- A visit limit, which limits the number of times the holder may enter a casino in Singapore.

- Helplines and counselling for problem gamblers and their families. For more information, visit the Singapore National Council for Problem Gambling website at www. ncpg.org.sg.

However, the best way to resolve the effects of problem gambling is, pardon the expression, between your ears. No host or safety measure can make up for a lack of prudence and responsibility on your part — and this applies to whales and ordinary folk alike.

So if you want to try it out for yourself, be my guest. Just keep in mind to set aside what you are willing to lose, and never drain personal savings or other funds to do so.

Want my job?

My move into casino marketing was a "lateral" one, which is a fancy term for moving from one field (or company) to a similar position in another. That's not the case for most people, who enter this field the same way as any other, from entry level. They begin as line workers in casinos to receive and entertain guests, making sure their day-to-day needs are met.

All this while, the sales and marketing team observes the new hires, identifying those with potential — those with enough charisma or good looks to form a good rapport with clients. They're then invited to try out for a sales position. Otherwise, it takes longer as you have to rise up the ranks through your own hard work.

Either way, it can mean many years of "menial" service, filling requests that seem insignificant or even unreasonable. But remember that a single bad customer experience can cost millions. Don't be fooled by the glitz and glamour, because a lot of drudgery goes on behind the scenes — all the usual cooking, cleaning, maintenance, stocking and accounting needs to get done, and to a very exacting standard.

CASINOS: LOSING, WINNING AND SO MUCH MORE

Many people want to enter the sales field. We may play up the benefits, like the money we make, or the generous tips (if we're allowed to accept them) — but remember, a lot of it comes from commissions, so we constantly need to close sales, besides being the go-to people for anything clients need. Our basic salary is not so different, and entering the field, you trade shift work for a 24-hour on-call period that rarely allows you time off.

To trade service for sales is to exchange safety and stability for stress and risk. Some people (like myself) like it that way, but it's certainly not for everyone. You're expected to think on your feet, and you live and die by split-second decisions made a thousand times every day. I'll say more about finding a role suited to your abilities later.

The sales numbers also hang over our heads, like the sword of Damocles. If you don't make them, the boss will demand an explanation. But in a service job, you're okay if you just do it right.

Even if a senior sales representative takes you on, it's no guarantee of success. Sadly, too few newcomers in the casino trade get good guidance, because their ostensible mentors are too busy, and rarely take the time to delegate or share their knowledge. For them, it's gaining new clients first, making existing clients happy second, and training new salespeople a very distant third. It's an easy pattern to fall into.

Few casinos invest in sales training. Even fewer give new salespeople meaningful responsibilities and clients to manage. I was fortunate enough to work for one that does;

for the majority, it is down to your own initiative and hard work to learn the trade

In a sales role, you effectively put yourself — and your time — at the mercy of others. Your time is no longer your own and you'll be on call most of the day. Will your family support that?

Furthermore, you're at the beck and call of clients, and in the casino trade, such clients will be millionaires and billionaires. Not all their requests will be possible, so it's crucial to say no gracefully.

But the rewards, if you attain them, are great. I've had the advantage of making friends with, and learning much from, the movers and shakers of various industries. You can read their bios, but imagine how much more you can learn in direct conversation with them!

Of course, they're human, and our friendship has privileged me to help them through many difficult times as well. I still remember the client who called me at 1.30 am, sobbing as he told me about his impending divorce from his wife. I dropped everything to visit him in Hong Kong to keep him company. He was grateful, and remains a good friend.

It's episodes like that that remind me why I do what I do — and illustrate the lengths a good salesperson must sometimes go to.

What we've learnt

1. Gambling isn't simply a vice. Thanks to integrated resorts, it's an experience you can sell alongside tours, hotel stays, theatre shows and many other attractive activities.
2. If you yourself must gamble, do it right and keep your greed in check. Your primary role is to help your customers get the best possible experience.
3. Being a salesperson means giving up safety and stability for an unpredictable, round-the-clock experience that brings both increased risk and greater rewards. It's certainly not for everyone.
4. Be prepared to build the relationship by the means available to you — even if you must be ready to help clients out at odd hours.

3

The Foundations of Salescraft

You see this watch? ... That watch cost more than
your car. I made $970,000 last year. How much did
you make? You see, pal, that's who I am, and you're
nothing. Nice guy? I don't give a shit. Good father?
Fuck you! Go home and play with your kids. You
wanna work here? Close!
— Alec Baldwin, in *Glengarry Glen Ross* (1992)

David Mamet's film *Glengarry Glen Ross* is a darkly funny
look at the goings-on in a real estate office, and brings out
the incredible pressure its salesmen are under to get as
many deals closed as possible, whatever the cost to themselves. In an early scene, a sales trainer played by Alec Baldwin drops by to give them a pep talk — if "pep talk" can also
mean "crude, psychopathic rant".

"You can't close the leads you're given? You can't
close shit. You *are* shit!" Baldwin thunders to the terrified

salesmen, who are trapped in the room with him and their uncaring boss.

"The leads are weak," a salesman protests.

"Fuckin' leads are weak? *You're* weak!" Baldwin shoots back. "I can go out there tonight, the materials you got, make myself $15,000! Tonight! In two hours!"

Baldwin's speech has endured both because we react so strongly to being told off like this, and the fact that his message, however rudely delivered, is exactly right. Whether the product is real estate, cars, insurance plans or yes, casino experiences, the end of all our efforts is a closed sale. A good salesperson closes better deals more frequently than an average one.

Make no mistake. *Everything* we're given — leads, mentorship and training — is so we can close more deals, and faster. As Baldwin put it: "Because only one thing counts in this life! Get them to sign on the line which is dotted!"

Do your strategies work?

We've all been at meetings where prospects quibble over minor details, stall for time or back out altogether. We've all seen promising deals crash and burn over what we thought were trivialities. Over time, it's easy to become discouraged and burnt out, and I've seen that happen to many good marketers, whether they work with whales or ordinary people.

The sales philosophy I subscribe to is very simple. Because our customers are the end-all of our business, we have to be careful to only take on those who are most likely to give it to us. We decide how much time, effort and money to spend on them. Eventually, your customer base will follow the Pareto Principle — most of your income will come from a small percentage of your customers. It is that small number you will form the deepest relationships with, but who they are takes much time and prospecting to discover. Like a miner testing his haul for gold, you'll need to evaluate each customer as you grow your relationship with them.[4]

That's why this book doesn't just give you a few sales hacks to try; it gives a planned approach with a definite beginning, middle and end. In any other field, a business opportunity is only pursued after careful planning, a strengths-and-weaknesses analysis and a study of all the risks involved. Notice what this doesn't contain: wishing, hoping or stalling. Everything you do should be a strategically planned action with a clear objective.

The end goal is the close of the sale. But there are many intermediate stages — the initial referral, the first meetings and the follow-up. Each of these represents a milestone that your sales relationship needs to reach before the close is in sight.

Often, there are problems because our goals are in conflict. The salesperson wants to generate interest in the product, make a clear and effective presentation, haggle over the details, and finally close. However, the prospect is thinking very differently — he wants to be sure he is getting the best deal possible before he commits. If the salesperson doesn't have anything worth buying, the prospect would like nothing more than for him to disappear forever.

Don't believe me? Try walking by a trade roadshow set up at any bus interchange or MRT station in Singapore. There are representatives whose sole duty is to stop you and sell you a credit card, insurance plan or what have you — and if you don't see a need for it, you can't get away quickly enough!

"Fuckin' leads are weak? You're weak!" is Baldwin's crude but effective way of putting forward a great truth: there are no bad prospects, only bad salespeople. Before a prospect can become a customer, it takes a good salesperson to ascertain what he wants, why he wants it and the best way to meet his needs. It's indeed true that not every prospect can be reached, but a good salesperson does his very best to truly confirm that.

The sales process is a dance. But you're not the one dancing — you're the maestro, the choreographer. No, the dance partners are your company and the client. Your role is to set them up, introduce them to each other and get them learning the steps so the dance happens... and both partners want it to happen again.

To that end, the success of the sales process depends on three high-level factors:

- Your attitude. Are you willing to constantly meet new people, learn what you can, and do everything in your power to give them the best experience that you and the company are capable of?

- Your behaviour. Do you show yourself to be passionate, enthusiastic and memorable, with full belief in and knowledge of your product?

- Your technique. Do you communicate and plan well, and use the right methods to prospect and close the sale?

The approach I have fine-tuned for many years now rests on these basic foundations:

- The result we want is a repeat customer, not just a closed sale. We are selling an experience that involves everyone, from the CEO to the service member on the floor. Teamwork is crucial across the entire organisation, not just our own small part of it.

- Build your sales team well, matching roles to personality, character traits and communication style. I simplify everything into two kinds of roles — Hunters and Gatherers. Both are critical, and a sales team that loses either cannot function. Those with a more proactive, outgoing personality type make better Hunters, while those with gifts for administration and attention to detail are needed as Gatherers. Most importantly, each team member must know (and be satisfied) that their role is in keeping with their personality.

- There is nothing mystical about attracting the client. Regardless of what they want, there are structured, systematic approaches that will greatly increase your chances of taking them on. Sales success is not inborn; it can be learned with strategy and hard work. The processes of closing sales in the casino trade are simply novel applications of tested principles.

- Clients are human beings first, with aspirations and wants just like you and me. Think of them as people to befriend, not walking, talking bank accounts. But at the same time, never let your guard down. Friendship may make business easier, but it's still business. A closed deal should benefit both parties, not stack everything in one side's favour.

- Provide clients with what they want, but keep the company's resources in mind. Learn to say no with grace, while keeping the client's friendship. Don't commit above your authority.

In a nutshell: Learn what customers want, as people and potential friends. Learn the best way you can provide it with your own personality, resources and skill set. And finally, deliver it in a way that shows you care about them. The marketer's role is not to convince the customer to hand over the cash, but to work with the customer in creating an experience they will happily pay for again and again.

I'll expand on these points in the subsequent chapters. But bear in mind that this advice is not for everyone. It will be hard, challenging work, and it may be a long time before you gain the skills and experience needed — and even longer before it truly pays off, big time. Until then, you will just have to grow, learn and enjoy the smaller wins that come your way.

If you're still eager to enter a sales role, congratulations! You're now better informed than the majority of newbies, and well on your way to catching your first whale.

Let's get started.

What we've learnt

1. As a salesperson, your aim is to close better deals faster.
2. Sales is a team effort and needs good co-operation and strategy. Everything you do should be part of an overall plan.
3. Your role is to work with the customer to create an experience that they will enjoy, and that the company can provide.
4. Learn the role that is best suited for your personality, and the best way you can build good relationships with the customers you serve.
5. Play the long game, and keep learning and growing. Don't be discouraged — over time, the closure process will become easier and easier.

PART TWO
IT'S ALL ABOUT
THE CUSTOMER

4

Hunters and Gatherers

> Whatever your situation, though, you should bounce
> around from casino to casino, rather than sticking
> with one host in one casino — unless, of course,
> it's me.
>
> — Steve Cyr[5]

I once knew a very capable casino administrator, who had
run things in our Melbourne facility for 20 years. He knew
and served the customers very well. With him, they were
welcomed, housed, fed and able to enjoy themselves like
clockwork. On the rare occasions when a customer com-
plained, he was always there to clean things up.

Then an opportunity came for him to be promoted.
He accepted, and so to Singapore he came to oversee our
operations.

Sadly, he couldn't make the numbers. Eight months
later, sales were down, morale was low and he was out
the door. What he had not realised was that the new job

needed him to proactively hunt down new customers, creating new business conditions rather than just reacting to them.

This person was one of our insiders, a professional in his own field, who had been unable to transition well to another. His departure taught us a lesson. No matter how much experience you have, it cannot overcome being put in the wrong job for your personality!

Other people are like wild horses, full of hunger and potential. If they are intelligent enough to find the right customers, it will show in their ability to build connections and bring other people to their point of view. If they can be brought on board and "tamed", so much the better. In fact, I prize such people above their educational qualifications — most of my team are degree holders, but once in a while I make an exception when I see someone hungry and capable enough. After all, *I* didn't have a degree when I started in this business!

At its simplest, a casino sales team can be divided into Hunters and Gatherers. Every tribe needs both Hunters to go out into the field, lay traps and bring in the game; and a team of people I call "Gatherers" to ensure it is properly cooked, prepared and distributed so the entire tribe eats well.

Both are equally important. In my team, I need both Hunters like myself who can increase sales and convince customers to join us; and Gatherers to ensure the insurance paperwork, records, checks and other administrative work gets done — and customers are kept.[6] Basically, in casino sales a Hunter acquires new customers and tends the relationship, while a Gatherer ensures they remain our customers.

How to join my team

You've probably heard the fable of a talented young violinist who dreamt of playing in the great concert halls of the world. One day, he got the opportunity to play before a great virtuoso. But after that performance, the virtuoso simply said, "You lack the fire," and walked away.

Disheartened, the violinist stopped playing and never touched the instrument again. Many years passed, until one day he ran into the virtuoso again at a function.

"You made me give up on my dream," he said, recounting the story as the bitterness and anger he'd felt came rushing back. "All I needed was a bit of encouragement — but you destroyed it!"

"Oh, I tell everyone that," said the virtuoso. "It's what they do next that reveals whether I was right or not."

Like the virtuoso, we're looking for fire, and those candidates that truly have it will display it — first at the interview, then the appointments they have.

You can't fake it, but you can fail by hiding it when it's not supposed to be hidden. Here's how to make it show through.

There are two ways to secure an interview with me, or some other team leader. Either write a brilliant CV I can't put down, or be referred by someone I know. Like any busy manager, I assume that a referral means the candidate comes pre-vetted. I can't look at every CV sent to me, so I rely on people I trust to send prospects my way.

But I don't just vet the candidate — I vet the referee. If a candidate who is introduced to me does badly, it reflects poorly not just on himself, but the person who sent him!

Here's my advice for the attitude you should bring into interviews:

1. Conversational judo
This is the way I structure job interviews for prospective team members: It might be a ratio of five casual questions to one serious one, with the conversation seamlessly shifting in and out of various topics. "How was your day?" I might ask. "Nice dress you're wearing." Then after some light banter, a serious question: "What do you think about political regulation of casinos?"

After that I lighten the mood. "Nice shoes. Do you polish them?" Then I repeat the process, seeing how fast they can think on their feet while maintaining confidence and presence of mind.

2. Gung-ho hunger and determination
How do you know when someone you talk to is truly passionate and determined to go the distance? When their eyes shine and their voices come alive with purpose; when there's a depth to their words and a resolve in their conviction; when they've done their homework and the knowledge they have gathered springs forth.

To be passionate is to have discovered what you were meant for, and prepared yourself accordingly. Present that to the interviewer, and you'll have gone a long way.

3. Professional problem-solving with or without me

I want to know how you'll handle a dicey sales or experience situation.

Despite everyone's best efforts, mishaps can and do happen. One customer got so incensed that he hurled a plate at his wife's head! It struck her so hard that she was stunned.

Big risk, big drama

Unfortunately, the rush of gambling sometimes brings out the worst in people — rich or poor.

One of my customers tended to get angry and throw ashtrays at the dealer if he lost the game. The dealer learned to duck when one came his way, but one day a new dealer took his place. And on that day, the customer's aim was particularly good.

The ashtray struck the poor dealer full force, and cut his face open! Blood poured out through the gash, and we had to get him emergency treatment. He wanted to press charges. In the end, we mediated between them and were able to negotiate a settlement. The customer paid the dealer an undisclosed sum, and the matter was settled.

Other times, angry customers damage casino property. We always knew when one of them had lost three hands in

For an instant, everyone was still. There was a $300,000 live bet on the table, but no one noticed — we were all watching what the customer would do next. No one wanted to be the next to get hit by a flying ashtray!

Why do I bring this up? I want to know the potential hire's priorities and thought processes. Will you approach the customer, tend to his wife or restart the game as if nothing happened?

And how will you handle the egos of everyone involved in a smooth and professional way? Ignoring the customer's tantrum sends the message that you tolerate this kind of

a row; he would rip his cards into confetti and hurl his chips and drinks to the floor. When that happened, we would pick up the ripped cards and tape them back together, clear the chips and clean up the broken glass.

During the 20-minute wait, the customer would cool off. We'd read the score off the ruined cards and replace the deck, and then continue as if nothing had happened.

When dealing with such situations, keep these two principles in mind:

1. Property can be replaced. Relationships cannot. If bad behaviour can be pacified or put up with, do it in a constructive and non-argumentative way.

2. Put your ego aside and de-escalate conflict quickly. Even if the customer is in the wrong, it will serve no purpose to argue with him in front of other guests.

behaviour, but calling security would affect everyone else's experience.

My solution is to treat and de-escalate. I would take charge of the situation immediately, sending someone to tend to the customer's wife while I pacify him. I let it take as long as it needs; we can always run another game.

Not every situation is so violent. How would you approach a customer who's lost everything and is contemplating suicide? What would you do if a customer is genuinely angry and hurling out one "fuck you" after another because a waiter spilled his drink, the room he wants isn't available or he's just having a string of bad luck? What if an important item goes missing from his hotel room? All these things can happen, and you need to display the temperament to take it in your stride.

It isn't my interview style to be rude and offensive, but others might deliberately try to rile you up to see how you respond.

What's in your bones?

For me, a ratio of three Hunters to one Gatherer is ideal. Both sets of responsibilities require very different kinds of people, and only very rarely have I met someone who is able to fill both roles. I respect people who know themselves well enough to remain in the right positions, even if it means turning down lucrative opportunities.

On one occasion, before I knew of this distinction, I invited an up-and-comer to join my sales team. He had done his service job fantastically. I not only needed a new sales-person, I needed someone who could handle the adminis-trative side of things, like filing reports. "Why don't you join my team?" I asked him.

"No, Marcus. I can't."

I couldn't believe my ears. "Why not? I'm giving you an opportunity here!"

He stuck to his guns. "I don't drink, smoke or like to talk to others. I'm an introvert and would rather stay at my desk."

So I let him go, and he remained as a Gatherer. The last I heard of him, he was doing extremely well — strategising the casino layout, working out where to place gambling tables, slot machines and other things. He is a clear reminder that above all, you need to know your strengths.

The best Gatherers are calm, almost cold-blooded specialists, able to stay composed and execute the plan no matter what. On the other hand, the Hunter is a Jack of all trades, thinking on the fly, aggressive and proactive, savvy and resourceful. For instance, what if a new prospect gives you just five minutes to make your pitch? You need to think on the spot. You need to hook him and reel him in within just a few seconds.

Or suppose you must take him to a nightclub, com-plete with drinks — all of that on the company's tab. Can you keep your wits about you? Will you remember it's still a client-business relationship? When you're told, "I want a private jet flight. I want half a million dollars in credit, and free food and drinks," will you still be able to negotiate on the company's behalf? All these perks cost the company money, and your bosses need to be sure the revenue he provides will make up for that.

Because of the large sums of money that each marketer can gain or lose, I believe that emotional intelligence is more than just the most important part of the job; for the Hunter, it *is* the job. Awareness of your own emotional state and personality must combine with awareness of the client's needs, moods and words to produce a response within a few seconds; one that leads the client to accept what you have to offer. In stressful situations, the best response must come immediately, instinctively. It's not what you have in your head, but in your bones.

I'll focus more on Hunters because I'm one myself, but Gatherers will also benefit from what I have to share. In this and many other businesses, a close friendship with customers isn't optional. It's a necessity.

What we've learnt

1. A sales team needs both Hunters and Gatherers. Each role needs a different personality type, so you need to know which one you can be.
2. Surprises can happen. We simulate them in interviews, so prepare accordingly by understanding how to deal with them. Remember, put people above possessions, and de-escalate conflicts quickly.
3. A sales role *requires* you to actively tend to your relationships with customers, so that you can form close friendships and gain their trust.
4. Each sales meeting needs you to be fully alert and on your toes. Keep the company's needs in mind, and be careful what you commit to. It's not what's in your head, but what's in your bones.

5

Whales:
A Field Guide

> If we are so contemptibly selfish that we can't radi-
> ate a little happiness and pass on a bit of honest
> appreciation without trying to get something out
> of the other person in return — if our souls are no
> bigger than sour crab apples, we shall meet with
> the failure we so richly deserve.
> — Dale Carnegie, *How to Enjoy Your Life & Your Job*[7]

The old master of persuasion and friendship, Dale Carnegie, once booked the same New York hotel ballroom every year to hold a series of lectures. However, one season, after the guests had been invited and the tickets printed, the hotel management dropped a bombshell on him.

A letter from the manager told him they were now demanding *three times* the rental rate from before. Naturally, Carnegie did not want to pay the increased rate, and neither would his clients.

But pointing out what *he* wanted would not have done any good. Instead, Carnegie went to see the manager and even agreed with where the manager was coming from! "If I were in your position," Carnegie said, "I should probably have written a similar letter myself."

Carnegie went on to produce a sheet of paper, and drew two columns on it: Advantages and Disadvantages. Then he pointed out the advantage of the rate increase and his departure — the hotel would of course earn far more revenue by hosting dances and conventions than it would have by hosting his lectures. It would be more profitable in the short term if Carnegie held his lectures elsewhere.

But doing so held two disadvantages for the hotel. First, its far steadier and more regular income from Carnegie's organisation would be wiped out, and second:

These lectures attract crowds of educated and cultured people to your hotel. That is good advertising for you, isn't it? In fact, if you spent five thousand dollars advertising in the newspapers, you couldn't bring as many people to look at your hotel as I can bring by those lectures. That is worth a lot to a hotel, isn't it?

Without any more petitioning, he left the sheet of paper (and the final decision) with the manager. The next day, he learnt that his rent had only been increased by 50 percent, not 300 percent.[8]

Approach the sale from the customer's point of view,

and show the benefits to him, not yourself. Think of yourself less as a company representative and more of a good friend who understands what he needs and is full of great recommendations on how to have an amazing time.

The customer experience

Let's get one platitude out of the way: "The customer is always right." This saying, however well-intentioned, usually does more harm than good.

Poorly informed managers take it to mean: "Agree to any customer demand, however rude, ill-founded or unreasonable." The result? Poorly motivated staff who know that a rude or abusive customer complaint will mean their managers instantly take the customer's side against them.

What makes this myth so deadly is that it does contain a little bit of truth. A business *does* exist to serve its customers, because the customer experience is an enormous part of its survival. We want our customers to have a good time. We want to meet whatever need we're entrusted to meet, and do it well. But it is precisely because of this that we cannot say yes to everything. Instead, we can say, "Here is something better — why not try it?" Only in very rare (and regrettable) circumstances do we part ways, and even then, we do our best to part as friends.

We want our customers, in short, to want what we're selling. It's the way Apple revealed the iPhone to the world — with Steve Jobs creating a new need, and convincing the world they actually wanted to fill it.

Generally, it's much harder to attract new customers than it is to keep existing ones. Gaining goodwill with my customers — through patience, honesty and showing that I truly care for them — is crucial in their decision to stay with me and trust me, despite any unpleasant experiences they might have had. If I hadn't done that homework, it would have cost the company not only millions of dollars, but also the priceless respect of 40 top customers. *That* is the core of the Chinese concept of *guanxi*, or mutual respect and trust.

This principle holds, regardless of whether we are offering taxi rides or private jet flights, fast food or Michelin-starred dining, plain water or champagne. The rich are often very exacting with their demands, and don't have time to argue — they can simply take their business elsewhere. However, there is a very strong flip side. Once you've gained their trust and confidence, they are very likely to support you through almost any problem or difficulty you may encounter.

The first step is to learn what *they* want. Finance and productivity guru Ramit Sethi applies this to dating:

A friend of mine had a crush on one of my friends, a big-name, top-tier guy. She was mystified that he didn't seem to be into her, and she asked for my advice... I said one thing: "What kind of woman does a man like him want?"

She responded with generic BS: "Confident, smart, blah blah."

I said, "Ok, just stop. This dude is a high-caliber

man. He is SWIMMING in women. Of course he wants that — but that's just the price of admission. What else?"

She was stumped — and admitted she'd never really thought of what HE would want — because in her mind, for her entire life, she'd been the prize that men pursued.[9]

You're polished and professional — but likewise in reaching the ultra-rich, that's just the "price of admission". Now the real work of selling yourself begins.

Every day, all of us must decide how to parcel out our time and attention. The ultra-rich face this problem tenfold — they must screen requests from their families, shareholders, the media and a million other places. Without the clearance of a secretary, yours may not even be looked at.

In this chapter, I will show how the principle of customer-focused marketing really works on the ultra-rich, and how to get appointments that begin with them truly wishing to see you. But before I do, my advice is to get to know yourself first, and how to handle the appointment when it does come your way.

At the risk of replacing one tired cliché with another, let me say instead: "The customer's *experience* is your priority." This means that the customer's input is treated with great respect, and our goal is to consider how best to meet their requests, spoken or unspoken, with the resources and skills we can provide.

This is where the skill of emotional intelligence comes in — reading past words and manners to get at someone's inner thoughts and feelings, and responding in a constructive way that is both true to yourself *and* tailored to the client's personality. As we'll see, this affects the entire approach of the conversation and the kind of questions and concerns that the customer will raise.

What whales truly want

> Where can I talk about my problems and other people won't say, "You've got a lot of money, bitch, bitch, bitch"? I do have a lot of money, but I still have problems. Sure, they're high-class problems, but they're still problems.
> — Leslie Quick III[10]

In his book *The Thin Green Line*, wealth columnist Paul Sullivan relates his meeting with investment group Tiger 21, a monthly meeting of high-net-worth business leaders worth at least $10 million and willing to pay a $30,000 annual membership fee. They meet in person once a month to discuss their investments — although as Sullivan later reveals, it's less of a discussion than a brutally honest teardown.

The four wealthy businessmen he meets at the beginning of the book are arguing not about stock tips or finances, but their origins. "I was listening," he writes, "to four men worth tens of millions of dollars argue over who had the poorest childhood."[11] Imagine several of the richest men in the country bickering over that!

Generally, the majority of whales have rags-to-riches stories — that is, they truly *earned* the fortune they now have. They took enormous risks to get to their position, and they are still responsible for the smooth in- and outflow of billions of dollars.

But on a day-to-day basis, such "earners" are bored. They can literally wake up $1 million richer than they were the night before. Gone is the uncertainty, the fear that their venture might not work out, the mental rehearsal of what they're going to tell their shareholders should it all go south.

"I want risk. I want excitement," they think — and so they go to the casino. They want a new risk to take on, a new challenge to conquer. They are like the mountaineer who keeps scaling one peak after another. If they can get that thrill by trying to break the bank at our casinos, they're more than welcome to take a crack at it.

I'm not exaggerating in the slightest. I once met one of my biggest clients at the gambling table, and chatted him up. "Are you having fun, Mr X?" I asked. "You're not betting a lot." I knew his net worth, and was aware he could bet much more than that if he wanted.

"Marcus, I'm against the market every single minute of the day. Why should I take on more risk?"

I laughed. "Mr X, you can put in the maximum bet of $500,000. It's nothing to you."

But he wasn't looking for big winnings — he was looking for fun. "What's fun for me is that I can dictate the market," he said, then indicated the table. "But I can't dictate this bloody game."

That piqued my curiosity. "It's out of your control," I said. "You like that?"

"Profits don't matter. P&L statements don't matter," he answered.[12] "If I want a stock to rise, it rises. If I want it destroyed, it's fucking destroyed. But this bloody game... I can't do that. It flusters the hell out of me. *That's* where I get my fun."

I left him to enjoy himself. The day he wanted to bet more, I'd be there.

Earners have started or run great businesses, and so they grew up with risk, hard work and care for finances. As a result, they can look at you and see a kindred soul, enough to form a relationship with and support if they can. They understand what you're going through, and appreciate what you're doing — they might overlook certain faults, and give you chances to do more for them.

But don't take that for granted. They'll also be the fastest to shut the door if they smell a rat and think you're not being honest; they're streetwise and smart, and they can see deception coming a long way off.

Another key group of whales inherited their wealth. They're born into a more privileged background, and as such their sense of risk is less developed. Depending on their upbringing, they might have different attitudes towards gambling per se — but what's common is that they all want to have fun. One young customer blew US$50 million in two days, and just shrugged it off!

For inheritors, after I make friends with them, I don't go so much into persuading them to gamble. It's all about the experience — how much entertainment, gaming and happiness I can generate out of four or five days.

The good, the bad and the stingy

There is a group of whales that will *not* accept the risk to their fortunes no matter what. They track everything down to the cent, and on principle they often don't gamble. If they somehow grace a casino with their presence, they only put down very small amounts.

When we find that out, we rarely prospect them, although we do keep in touch and try to part as friends, as they might remain good sources of referrals or information. This is why I believe that time spent prospecting and building relationships is never wasted.

How to meet whales

Sometimes clients come to you looking to gamble and have a good time; others come looking to know you better before trusting you to manage their experiences in a casino.

But remember that time spent prospecting is never wasted. Even if a prospect has never gambled or even entered a casino before, that's no reason not to make friends with him. He might (a) be curious enough to try it for himself, or (b) know friends and associates you can reach out to.

Many whales have gatekeepers such as secretaries and security guards between them and anyone seeking to enter their presence — but all of those can be bypassed when a client who's had an amazing time with you recommends your services to those in his network. Who in his right mind runs a friend through the full gauntlet of secretaries and security checks?

Either way, don't simply wait for contacts to drop into your lap. Be proactive in going for, and organising, events so the whales end up coming to you. One of the benefits of working for a major chain is that the company will often do this. Creativity always helps, so if you have a truly creative proposal, there's no harm in suggesting and helping organise an event!

I'm a watch guy, so I love setting up watch events. Recently, I also did a tailoring event, in which we flew in the Italian master tailor of a major brand of men's suits. Many of my clients came in to get new suits made specially for them. It was an excellent opportunity to not only meet new prospects, but make a good first impression by giving them something they wanted and valued.

Informal meetings break the ice and open the door to deeper discussions later on. Think of it as a funnel. You'll likely meet, say, 50 new prospects at such an event. Of these, perhaps 10 will qualify for more time and effort getting to know them. Of those 10, one or two will be ready to become long-term clients right away! Others may need more persuasion, or may be willing to join your referral network and funnel even more prospects to you.

So get to know them first by thinking of something they want, and that the company can provide. The next step is

Boundaries and the sexes

> Lose money for the firm, even a lot of money, and I will be understanding; lose reputation for the firm, even a shred of reputation, and I will be ruthless. — Warren Buffett[13]

Short version: Never go to bed with any client. It's not worth it.

Long version: Many a marketer has bedded a client and lived to regret it, to the detriment of everyone involved. Sexual dynamics are very much in play, whether we realise it or not. Boundaries need to be respected, because this is business and all parties should keep a professional distance from each other. Friendship and becoming confidantes is good and even desirable, but even then there are limits.

There has never been a situation where sleeping with clients ended well. Everybody talks, and eventually word will get out. Trust me, you do not want to be in that situation, as it's a fast way to end up in the newspapers, tarnishing your company's and your own reputation forever.

Generally, interactions and ice-breaking between opposite sexes is easier, because of some degree of mutual attraction. But the ease of breakthrough is accompanied by a stronger need to draw clear boundaries.

In same-sex interactions, it is often harder to initially break the ice. Men and women seek on some level to compete with other members of their gender, and it often causes some friction at first. But with that comes more respect for mutual boundaries once you are comfortable with each other as friends and professional contacts.

Warren Buffett, one of the world's richest men, has a morality test we all ought to use: "Do nothing you would not be happy to have an unfriendly but intelligent reporter write about on the front page of a newspaper."[14]

to get to know them as friends, and learn more about their businesses, outlook and personality, and in doing so, size them up as prospects for you and your team. Finally — and this needs to be the last step — you sell them the experience you know they need for themselves and their families.

Such events are, at heart, opportunities to network and meet people far more intimately than via phone calls or emails. The whales are in your turf, unshielded by secretaries or employees. Why not say hi?

Becoming the go-to guy

A client once called me in a near-panic. "Marcus, my wife's watch is broken. Do you know anyone who can fix it?" I'm known in billionaire circles as the Fixer, and my reputation sometimes precedes me.

Clients and close friends know I'm a watch guy. I know all the brands and follow the market, and I love wearing, investing in and reading about luxury watches. So I naturally came to mind when he needed help with his wife's watch. I was able to send a driver to collect it and get his problem sorted out.

Now of course there were other people he knew who could've helped. It was because of our relationship and the impact I'd made that I got the call. I could be relied on to solve that problem right away because of the time I'd spent with him, and the trust I had built up.

That's the benefit of good conversations with clients. As time goes by, a relationship based on mutual trust and respect is built up. My clients now know not to bother me 24/7, because after we come to know each other well, I create boundaries; they come to understand my need for time to service them properly.

In other words, I endure some minor bother early on, so as to avoid more later.

In fact, this is echoed by property agent Shirley Seng, who made the news for earning a $1.5 million commission from selling a luxury penthouse. The profile of her in the *Straits Times* reads:

> And if there is one tip she could give in dealing with wealthy clients, Ms Seng advises: "Speed is crucial. I always try to get back to them within one to two hours. I want to let them know they are my priority."
>
> Ms Seng, who zips around town in a white, three-year-old Audi A4, said she also goes the extra mile for clients, such as picking them up in her car and dropping them off wherever they want to go. Sometimes she also helps them run errands.
>
> "Times are tough, unlike 10 or 20 years ago. Today's agents need to do more for their clients. But you need to do it with your heart, so they can feel your sincerity," she said.[15]

Know your customer, know yourself

One thing I love about the casino marketing business is that who you are and what you like are just as important as any

WHALES: A FIELD GUIDE

head knowledge you have about closing the sale. Every friendship and business deal is different. As a go-to guy, you need an understanding of your own likes, dislikes, strengths and weaknesses. If you have insider information about a client's hobbies, that's a great ice-breaker. If they are into the stock market and you can have great conversations about it, that's always a plus.

For instance, I don't play golf — I've never come to like it — but one of my staff members is a keen golfer and uses that to build connections with his clients. They talk about the best golf courses in the world, and because he knows the game intimately and speaks the language, they take him seriously when he recommends a course (and casino) in say, Melbourne. "You should really try it," he says — and they do!

Start with who you are, and don't try to be someone you're not. For instance, someone who picks up golf just for the deals he can make on the course will be spotted for what he is almost immediately, as will someone who truly loves the game and is at ease playing it. Guess which one clients prefer?

The idea is to find common ground so you can easily speak their language. Identify what your passions are, then try others to see if you really like them. Make sure you're learning more about not only your clients, but yourself — every day. Remember also that if you're a Gatherer, don't try to be a Hunter — and vice versa.

"But Marcus, what if I don't like anything to do with the high life?" I've been asked.

Then consider what you *do* know. Do you know of any great wonton noodle places right here in Singapore? Any Japanese restaurants? Many, many people love talking about food, drinks and companionship, so those make great starting points. Others are into philanthropy, the arts or sports, so look out for such associations in your research.

Alternatively, think back to what they have said during interviews with the media, and try to find common ground with their values and guiding principles. For instance, if they mention that they are more introverted, that's the cue for the introverts among you to discuss how that particular trait has helped them in everyday life.[16] Every little bit helps, and you might become a go-to person in a way that surprises both of you!

On the other hand, if there is truly no common ground, that should have been clear in your background research. In cases like these, it helps to refer the prospect to a team member you know can work with him.

In the following chapters, I'll discuss initial meetings, the different kinds of whales and other principles in more detail. I certainly don't have the final word on every encounter you'll have, but the strategies I outline should be adaptable enough to attract and captivate anyone — provided, of course, you keep your wits and think fast. Good luck!

What we've learnt

1. Approach sales from the customer's point of view, not your own. What's important is what matters to *him*, not you.
2. Understand the different types of whales. Generally, earners seek risk and thrill, while inheritors want a good time with plenty of fun.
3. Meet whales and get to know them via informal events that give them something they want.
4. Start by building relationships, finding common ground and learning more about each prospect. The sale only enters the picture *after* a strong friendship has been built.

6

Selling the Dream — Quickly and Often

Theirs is a firmament of 35-person entourages, flown in to Las Vegas on business jets, private aircraft, or chartered jumbos. They're shuttled by fleets of stretch limousines — stocked with Dom Perignon and Beluga caviar — to places such as the Mansion at MGM Grand, among the world's most exclusive accommodations. There, concierges, VIP hostesses, casino hosts, casino executives, limo drivers, butlers, personal chefs, and hookers cater to their every whim.

— Deke Castleman, *Whale Hunt in the Desert*[17]

What's the difference between the successful and everyone else? It's not how much time, money or energy they have — we all have 24 hours a day, money can be made whenever you're willing to work hard, and energy well-managed goes a long way.

The difference is that the successful have a dream, and their time, money and energy are spent in pursuit of that dream. It's the reason they're alive, the reason they get up in the morning, the reason they exhaust themselves reaching out, hustling and closing. They eat, sleep and breathe their work.

Consider the fact that whales aren't usually defined by their personal characteristics, but by the companies they have built or transformed. Despite his stepping down from the top job, Bill Gates is Microsoft; the late Steve Jobs was Apple; Jack Ma is Alibaba, and so on. Their realised dreams define who they are.

Most of the whales we work with are precisely that kind of hardworking, hard-charging business leader, or are being groomed to be their successors. As they gain more and more, they turn their thoughts to the possibilities that open up to them. The struggling small business owner knows his fantasies of dating Britney Spears are just that — fantasies. But when he expands, grows his empire and has a few million dollars he doesn't know what to do with...

- "I want to watch an NBA game from a front-row seat."

- "My daughter *loves* One Direction. Can she get a front-row seat at their concert and meet them backstage?"

- "My wife wants a Paddock Club pass at the Singapore Grand Prix, and a meeting with Sebastian Vettel. Can you help?"

71

That's where we come in. Our job is less selling ourselves than it is making their dreams a reality. We guess and learn what they want, then offer to use our connections to make it happen. Sometimes they don't even realise what they truly want till we tell them!

For instance, no one admits they actually want to go to a Victoria's Secret fashion show and meet the Angels. You could just casually ask, "Do you know Victoria's Secret?"

"Of course I do," they say. If they are being polite, they don't continue with, "Do you think I'm stupid?" (Of course, some do; but part of this job is growing a thick enough skin not to take it personally.)

"What if I told you... I have two passes to the Victoria's Secret fashion show in New York?" You'll see their faces light up! "And," you add, "they're good for the after-party. Fancy meeting some Angels?"

"Oh my God. What do I have to do to get that?"

"Well, why don't you come down to our London hotel? Spend a few days with us, then we'll fly you on a round trip to NY."

It's not just Victoria's Secret. I've actually been told, "I want to give my wife a Hermes bag. She's been asking me every day!" Thanks to our connections with various luxury brands, we can make it happen. Then the conversation becomes not about justifying the sale to the customer, but working with the customer to make what we both want happen.

Remember that dreams are not needs, but wants. Always be thinking to yourself: "How can I find out more about what the customer really wants, and how can I deliver that benefit with what my company provides me?" Persuade them in a structured way that lets them know the experience that awaits him, and what they have to do to truly enjoy it.

If you have become their friends, with the prep work I'll show you in Part Three, this is actually easier than you might think.

This will help you avoid the rookie mistake that Ramit Sethi calls the "I, I, I syndrome", the tendency to go on and on about what you yourself want. It may be important to you, but the customer doesn't care about that. It's both a turn-off and a huge waste of time.[18]

Focus on what the customer wants and how he will benefit from the experience. In fact, the *only* time when you can talk about your own wishes is when you've formed such a friendship that the whale closes the sale on your terms — simply because you two are such good friends. Even then, the customer should still see a clear benefit to himself.

Making the numbers

If you are truly sure you're made for the job, hang in there no matter how tough things get. The only true failure is giving up.

I firmly believe that with the right skills, teamwork and plans, no target is impossible to meet. That's the attitude you should have going into any new effort, especially when you see what is expected of you in the coming year.

Let's say my annual target is a $4 billion turnover. It's a huge target. The number of zeroes might paralyse a newcomer. But let's break it down. For a year's turnover of $4 billion, it represents a rounded-off monthly turnover of $334 million. Given how many high-net-worth customers we attract, it seems doable if we manage a high closure rate.

Now divide this by four to get a weekly turnover. We're looking at a sum of just $83.5 million each week. Doesn't seem so big now, does it?

But given the nature of the business, with peak and lull periods, we can manage with less if we're sure the peak period can make up for it. During a lull, a week with only $75 million turned over is a good one. But during a peak, like Chinese New Year or the school holidays when everyone starts travelling, many of us manage to turn over $600 million in a single week!

My results have borne this out, month after month. I have the sales targets I do because I deliver on them — I matched my predecessor's turnover in my first year, and then made an enormous jump the next! Where other teams struggled to bring in even one new customer, I was welcoming as many as 20.

How did I do this? By building friendships first, then sales, and with whales not only from Singapore but around the world. I get them to commit for the long term — so they agree to make multiple trips every year. Each time they come, they bring friends and associates to enjoy themselves too. In short, I make sure that each customer comes in as a repeat visitor, and leaves as an ambassador. That way, they create turnover without our help!

What I am saying is that you have to plan things and break them down, then turn customers into revenue multipliers whenever possible. When I share this at training sessions, everyone is stunned!

But what if the target still seems out of reach? Even I have my limits. If I were asked to get a $10 billion turnover, I'd probably go, "Hey, up yours, man," with everyone else.

That said, such a situation where a target is truly out of reach is *very* unlikely. Here's why.

You see, your bosses have targets too, and they are accountable to their own bosses for yours and their performance. Your boss wants his bonus too, so your targets aren't just plucked from thin air and shoved down your throat. A truly unreasonable target would have been stopped by him long before. "$10 billion? We did only $2.5 billion last year!" he might say. "Why increase it by 400 percent?"

It was initially difficult for me to do that, and I made a lot of mistakes starting out. I had come from an entrepreneurial background, making hard decisions every day, managing people but with no one to report to. When I entered casino sales, I entered a world of bureaucracy, politics and power plays. My bosses seemed to be timid, afraid to take revenue-generating risks.

But were they just worried about themselves? Not at all! I was to learn that they coordinated with various other departments, and had to justify every decision each of us made. We had to prove our worth to the company, and my boss was the one who stood in front of the directors to make our case. The last person you want to mess around with is your boss, because your prospects in the company depend entirely on how he appraises you.

So before you criticise your boss, put yourself in his shoes and identify what he has to deal with. Do the same thing you would for a customer — learn what he wants, and help him to achieve it. He needs to manage the numbers, and so do you.

Everyone has bad days

Off target? Behind schedule? Stay positive instead of giving in to the pressure. No target is too big if you keep your wits and planning about you.

Positivity and optimism aren't just nice add-ons — the sales profession *demands* these things. You have to be self-motivated, and if you dread going to the office and are sick and tired of meeting people day in and day out, that's a sign that you need a break... or a role change altogether.

Everyone has down days, so I try my best to keep my team motivated and inspired. And I've found that the best way to do it is to knuckle down and put my own nose to the grindstone. "Oh shit, the boss is going all out and we're so far behind!" they think. Between that, appreciation for them and a pat on the shoulder to show I understand, it works!

Team loyalty, with everyone sticking together for better or worse, isn't something that happens by accident. It is made through the interactions and words we use each and every day.

The proactive Hunter: Putting it all together

I'm particularly proud of the way I attracted an Indian non-gambler I'll call Mr L, whom I first met at a real estate event in Hong Kong. (Investment events are where contacts are likely to come to you; mark out a few on your calendar every year.)

It started with an introduction to me from a mutual friend. "He's bloody rich," the contact told me, and gave me the name of the exclusive apartment complex where Mr L lived. We fell into conversation, and I learned that he loved cars and wine. It turned out we had a lot in common!

Mr L was a human resource professional, connecting large companies with high-level candidates for positions like CEO or CFO. In fact, if my company ever needed a new CEO, we'd have gone to him! He earned much from the hefty commissions that came his way.

But I held back and never mentioned my work. In the end I gave him my name card (it doesn't say I'm in the casino business), and in the months following the event, we remained in touch by SMS. When I was back in town I let him know, and we ended up getting coffee after two weeks, and lunch after a month. In the meantime, I learned everything I could about him.

All this while, we talked about what interested us — I didn't want to bug him too much, and was determined not to try to sell anything to him till he truly wanted it.

Why? Because I knew that everyone he met with had an agenda, and sooner or later, would go, "Will you buy something from me?" It's a burden all rich people carry; nobody simply becomes their friend for its own sake. They also fear you might ask for a stock tip, or a discount on their products and services.

I genuinely liked our conversations, but I wanted *him* to initiate the process of the sale — which he did in spectacular fashion before we met for the third time.

"Marcus, cut the bullshit," he said on the phone, frustration in his voice. "Cut the bullshit and tell me what you're selling to me."

"I'm not selling you anything, Mr L," I said. "Do I look like someone with something to sell?"

"No," he admitted.

"Do you think I'm trying to cheat you?"

At this point, we had come to like each other — the thought of me cheating him was inconceivable. "No, you're not."

"Right," I said. "Do you *really* want to know what I do?"

"Yes, I really want to know what the hell you do."

I laughed. "Hey, Mr L, screw you. Get a heli and come down to Macau for lunch with me. Then I'll show you *exactly* what I do. You want to know, right?"

His curiosity was piqued. "So you're gonna call me a heli?"

Which I did. Helicopter rides out of Hong Kong aren't cheap — about HK$7,000 to $8,000 — but by this point I knew we'd be making back way more than that.

At lunch, Mr L admitted, "You really confuse the hell out of me."

"Relax, Mr L. You'll know exactly what I do in five minutes."

After dessert I brought him down to the casino, where the long-hidden truth dawned on him. "Ah," he said. "You're a gambling man."

"Yes sir, that's right!" I told him. "I take care of ultra high-net-worth individuals. I give them what they need to enjoy themselves and have a good time. Our revenue is based on them gambling."

"I don't really gamble," he told me. "But I'd love to help give you business by pointing my friends to you."

Thanks to my research, I knew exactly what to say. "Why not try it for yourself, Mr L? Take a million Hong Kong dollars on us and see." I'd done a credit check and learned he lived in a HK$80 million apartment; he could easily afford to lose far more than that.

"Do you gamble?"

Sales in a field as rife with social disapproval as gambling always require subtlety and good friendship. No one responds well to someone they've just met asking, "So, do you gamble?" Regardless of whether they do or not, it's still like asking: "Do you womanise?" or "Do you do drugs?"

I don't care how many women a person surrounds himself with; he will never actually consider himself a womaniser. Similarly, asking someone about his gambling habits is a no-no until you have entered their inner circle. If they ask what you do before this point, just answer that you're a marketing executive — without revealing for whom, until they are fully receptive.

Had I baited him? Certainly not! We started as friends, and only when we firmly enjoyed each other's company did I recommend my own services to him. My number one rule is that before I sell to someone, I become his friend; we must truly like conversing before I reveal my work for the casino. The relationship comes first, then the sale. The specific details may vary, but that is the impression I make on new clients and referrals alike.

Mr L turned out to be a gift that kept on giving. I took him around to try the various games. He'd only heard of blackjack, and I had to pull him away from the table after he'd lost quite a sum. But by the end of the evening he'd tried his hand at baccarat, roulette and many others he'd never heard of.

After a few hours of play, he had lost $500,000 — but he wasn't deterred. By day's end, he'd won back $700,000! I had to persuade him to stop for the night, to cap off the day on a high note.

"Wow, this is fun!" he exclaimed. (I'm not sure how it happens, but the first time they enter a casino, people usually win a lot of money. It does get them hooked and coming back.)

He promised to return the next week, and as I write, he remains a regular visitor — to the tune of US$25 million each time!

What we've learnt

1. We don't sell a company; we sell an experience that customers want.
2. Focus on knowing them as people and becoming their friends, before drawing out their needs. Avoid talking too much about yourself or your needs until the relationship is strong enough.
3. Work alongside your bosses. Understand their duties and who they report to, so you become an asset to them.
4. Build team loyalty through setting a good example yourself, and appreciating everyone's hard work.

PART THREE
FORTUNE FAVOURS
THE PREPPED

7

The Right Impression

> Put [pick-up artists] on South Beach in Miami and
> any number of better-looking, muscle-bound bul-
> lies will be kicking sand in their pale, emaciated
> faces. But put them in a Starbucks or whiskey bar,
> and they'll be taking turns making out with that
> bully's girlfriend as soon as his back is turned.
> — Neil Strauss, *The Game*[19]

My mentor had an amazing way of getting into clients'
heads. "Young man," she said to me early on, "Before you
learn this job, you'll have to learn how to eat. Whom do we
eat with most of the time?"

"Very rich people," I said.

"How old are they?"

"Fifty-plus, maybe 60 or 70?"

"That's right. Aren't they probably going to die soon?"
Where was she going with this? "Yeah, that's right."

She looked at me triumphantly. "So what do they want?
To live a longer life, right? If they eat healthily, they'll do that.

Saves you the trouble of looking for new customers!"

A key part of attraction, as she knew very well, is subtly getting into clients' heads and giving them what they want. To this day, I ensure I eat healthily, and encourage older clients to do the same. "Let's have something simple to cleanse our bodies," I might say. They'll certainly appreciate it, and feel even better when everyone leaves the table feeling good, not bloated.

Another reason not to over-order is that it's *not* classy even if you finish it. If you don't, it sends the signal to clients that you won't finish what you started!

Checking restaurants out

Always take prospects to restaurants where you'll dine yourself. You *have* planned the meeting, haven't you?

The client's dining experience can make or break the deal, so you'll have to be assured that the restaurant can deliver the quality your clients want. Here's how I make sure a Chinese restaurant can do so.

Forget the daily special. Forget the menu. Forget whatever it's showing on those massive ads outside. The *real* indicator of a Chinese restaurant's culinary ability is the dim sum and steamed fish.

Try it by yourself first. Is the dumpling skin moist, soft and translucent, or dry and hard? The former means the chefs know how to control the steam to produce the right texture; the latter means they don't bother. Are the prawns powdery? It means the restaurant doesn't take pride in ordering fresh ingredients, or can't properly dispose of stale ones. Does the fish meat get stuck on the bone? Then it's either not fresh, or overcooked.

In fact, *any* restaurant manager worth his salt knows this. Order just dim sum and steamed fish, and a senior staff member will know you're not just another customer! I did exactly this once, and the restaurant sent a senior chef to my table to get my feedback.

Take it from me. A restaurant that cannot steam a fish properly has no business entertaining your clients — no matter what dish you order, be it roasted, braised or double-boiled. Go somewhere that handles it better.

The main point is that clients will go by their feelings, and if you can "get into their heads" and attract them to yourself, that's half the battle won. And because you care about their experience so much, you take them to the places with the very best food.

Peacock theory

Neil Strauss' bestselling book *The Game* is the story of his ascent to the very top of the pick-up artist world — a community where men share scripts, tips and strategies on meeting women in public places, charming them and eventually landing them in bed. One of his methods, learned from a freelance street magician, was "peacocking". As Strauss explains it:

Peacock theory is the idea that in order to attract the most desirable female of the species, it's necessary to stand out in a flashy and colorful way [...] the equivalent of the fanned peacock tail is a shiny shirt, a garish hat, and jewelry that lights up in the dark — basically, everything I'd dismissed my whole life as cheesy.[20]

It worked! When Strauss wore something that truly stood out, women interested in meeting him "had an easy way to start a conversation".

Develop your own signature style that charms your clients. Me, I'm perfectly at home in a loud suit and colourful dinner jacket. As for watches, I wear one studded with diamonds, to better make an impression with. I dress to get whales' attention, not please the style police. I want to both look good, *and* be remembered for it by those who matter.

And if you're going to reach clients, anything that makes you stand out and be remembered is a good one. I don't care if anyone thinks I'm tacky or crass — my results speak louder than I can. I say let them succeed in their own subtler way and draw more business than me, and then we'll talk.

If possible, I recommend getting speech and singing classes like Strauss did, to free his voice from the bad habits of speaking too fast and mumbling. Remember, it's not what you can do in the comfort of the office or your home, but what you do in front of new prospects, under pressure and with millions of dollars at stake.

Your models are the peacock and the chameleon. The

peacock is memorable and flashy, while the chameleon is camouflaged and nearly invisible. In other words, you have to be unique enough to be memorable (like the peacock), *and* adaptable enough to change conversation styles on the fly (like the chameleon). Every customer interaction is unique, so prepare to adapt accordingly.

The bottom line: You are the one who needs to attract and adapt to the customer, not the other way around.

The attraction of confidence

There's no such thing as a bad product or a lousy service; only a badly placed one. You need to be clear who your product or service serves, and take pride that it will do it well. It's a matter of delivering to the best of your ability.

I once watched a cleaner in a Vegas casino for some time. He made the place so spick-and-span, it was unbelievable. I was so impressed, I tipped him $100 on the spot!

He was shocked. "Sir, I've worked here for 15 years. You're the only one who's ever given me a tip!"

"You take pride in what you're doing," I told him. "I noticed you cleaning every single corner, every single ashtray. I appreciate that, taking pride in what you're doing."

How does that relate to our work in sales? Simple — it's a competitive world, and however hard you work, there will always be people telling you you're not good enough. I've been trash-talked to by both managers *and* customers.

There's no sugar-coating it. My managers have demanded, "Why are you so hopeless and stupid?" or "What kind of lousy deals are you closing?" My clients have also snapped, "Your place is rubbish. Why is service so slow?" or "Where does someone find good food in this dump?"

When that happens, take it in your stride and improve what you can. We all have room for improvement, but I'm here to tell you that whatever you're told, you need that basic confidence in yourself and your product — a confidence that no one can take away. Don't let insults or scoldings discourage you. If you can't convince yourself that you have something worth selling, how can you convince others?

One technique I use is to accentuate the positive, and ensure that good expectations win out over any inconvenience customers might face. Here's how I sell an experience in a country that's great to stay in, and one that's not so great.

Suppose I were marketing a Melbourne casino. What would I mention? The blue Australian skies, the pleasant weather, the tourist attractions and the cute koalas.

Would I tell customers that Australian immigration is often a pain in the ass to go through, that you might run into casual racism from people, or that most of the food there could be better? Of course not!

The second example is the Philippines, where I recently stayed in a resort with amazing food cooked by brilliant chefs who knew how to get it just right; who were among many friendly, understanding staff members. Everyone provided excellent service and made me feel so well cared for, my time there was a blast. (Not mentioned: The smell, dilapidation and the presence of so many cockroaches that they give you a spray can of Baygon for your room. I am not making this up.)

Think out of the box. Be creative, but set limitations; notice that I *never* say anything factually untrue. It's a matter of the image that is created in your customer's head, not the experience that you yourself have had.

The tripod of impression

Prepare your points and craft your narrative in advance, so that when the customer is finally interested, you can smoothly segue into the experience he will enjoy. Then when he is in your company, use your knowledge of his background and character to make sure he has the best possible time.

Notice that good impressions don't come by accident. The three components of good attraction must show you to be (1) concerned about them, (2) memorable and easily brought to mind and (3) professional and with great pride in your work. Plan ahead so that all these things come to the forefront.

Everything you do and say to customers is part of your narrative — an integral component of how you will be perceived and remembered. First impressions count, so make them good ones. Then show that you genuinely care for them through helping them when they need it.

This truly hit home for me when one of my guests was scheduled to spend 12 hours gambling in one of our casinos in Vegas. One of the perks was that we could fly him over to Arizona, where he enjoyed a helicopter tour of the Grand Canyon.

Unfortunately, he became dehydrated during the tour, and fell ill. His symptoms were so bad that he had to leave the casino floor after only 9 hours of gambling. Of course we waived the three unused hours, because his health and safety were more important than the letter of the contract. We're dealing with human beings here, not machines!

In fact, the people factor is so important that everything else you do rests upon it. That should be the bedrock of any sales business, and one that does not do its utmost to tend the relationship and work for the benefit of customers will — and should — fail.

What we've learnt

1. Make an outstanding, unforgettable impression. The more such experiences created at your meetings, the better.
2. Pay attention to every detail, and do work you can be rightly proud of.
3. Accentuate the positive and create favourable impressions. This is being clear about features and benefits, not being dishonest.
4. Genuine care for others cannot be faked. It must be real, and come through at the first meeting, the last and every one in between.

8

Do Your Homework

> The fight is won or lost far away from witnesses —
> behind the lines, in the gym, and out there on the
> road, long before I dance under those lights.
>
> — Muhammad Ali

I once met a car salesman who very "kindly" demonstrated what *not* to do at a sales meeting. If he'd been deliberately trying to piss me off and lose my sale, I doubt he'd have done anything differently! He worked at the Mercedes-Benz showroom I frequented, and took over because my regular salesman was busy.

"Hi, I'd like to buy an S-class convertible," I said.

"What's an S-class convertible?" he asked. "We don't have that."

"It's in the news, launching in two months," I said. "You mean you don't have information about it?"

"Oh, I've only heard of the coupe. I've never heard of this S-class convertible."

"Well, you should be bringing it in. When will it be here?"

"I don't know."

"How much will it cost?"

"I don't know."

At this point, I felt like writing a quick note to the car dealership — this salesman's salary would be better spent elsewhere. He could have kept my sale if he had excused himself with a "Let me get that information for you, sir" and done a simple search. His answers showed that he wasn't good enough at thinking on his feet to do that; or that he just couldn't be bothered!

Never let the words "I don't know" pass your lips. Nothing kills a sale faster than not knowing your products! It's not enough to know what you're selling right now; you need to be aware of what's coming up, and how to pre-empt customer questions.

How to think two steps ahead

The best salespeople answer questions even before they're asked. This isn't some mystical ability; it's the result of hard work that predates the conversation itself. I try to learn so much that 80 percent of the work is done even before we sit down to meet, and the meeting itself follows a pattern I direct and know from start to finish.

Some helpful questions you can ask yourself include:

1. Who is most likely to buy my product?
Be as specific as possible. How old are they? Where are they located? What are their dreams and aspirations?

If you have to deal with many different people, come up with some "archetypes", or broad categories that you will approach differently. For an example, refer to the previous chapter, where I divided whales into earners and inheritors, and by age group. Each group is looking for a very different experience!

This can be subdivided further, such as by value system and family unit. Is the whale a swinging bachelor; a family man with strong old-fashioned values who's bringing his wife and children; or a "wolf" who's romantically linked with various women? They have to be wooed and rewarded very differently.

Bear in mind that each client is not a stereotype, but an individual. But these are *archetypes* — generalised ideals with some grounding in reality. They are guides to help you craft the right approach and predict questions, not strict templates to follow. As you gain experience, you will become better and better at reading the subtleties and adapting them to match your clients.

2. What experience do I want them to have?

If you sell clothes, you might play up the coolness and comfort of the fabrics. If you sell cars, you play up the experience of driving it and the feeling of power, safety or saving the environment — depending on which aim the car seeks to achieve. You wouldn't sell a Lamborghini supercar the same way you would a Volkswagen SUV.

And if you're selling a casino, consider things from each archetype's point of view. How will the various facilities and features give each group clear benefits that fulfil their wants?

For instance, the bachelor would probably appreciate package offers for his friends, social escorts and discounted food and drinks, so he can enjoy the thrill of gambling without worrying about his companions. The family man may not gamble much himself, but his children or relatives might. To sell to him, play up the hotel area's entertainment, sports facilities or restaurants. As for the wolf, you could arrange shopping tours and special perks at luxury retailers around the host city — all with your company's connections.

Note that this thought experiment only needs to generate answers that are usable and help you communicate with your customers better; they don't have to be exactly right. Their role is to open up avenues of discussion so that conversation can flow.

3. How can I structure conversations well?

This requires you to know the various personality types. A helpful system is the DISC division, which measures Dominance, Influence, Steadiness and Compliance in different people. The system helps you identify the communication styles they use, get into their heads and gain their trust.[21] This is still theoretical — its purpose is to provide you with a framework you can use to understand the real-world interactions you will have with prospects and customers.

Study the various personalities, and consider how they view commitments, risks and rewards. A Dominant personality tackles problems head-on, so bring out the reward first. "Like to go to Victoria's Secret? Here's what you have to do."

An Influencer might respond better to: "Here's something that will benefit your entire family. You've all worked hard and deserve some fun, don't you?"

S personalities respond better to principles and logical proof. "Come with me and you'll have a great time. Did I mention I could fly you to New York to watch the Victoria's Secret fashion show?"

Those with strong C personalities will appreciate being told, "I need 10 minutes of your time. There's something I'd like you to see that you may be interested in." That signals when they need to be ready. Then by all means, drop the angelic experience onto their laps.

4. What questions will they ask, and how can I answer in a way that satisfies them?

This consideration is the entire point of product knowledge, and will help you plug holes in your understanding.

This is where your understanding of the product combines with that of your customers. Customers assume you're speaking from a position of expertise, so don't blow it by saying, "I don't know."

Instead, put yourself in the customer's shoes. Imagine you're looking to buy your own product, or visit your own casino. What sort of questions would you ask salespeople?

Let's bring this into other kinds of sales. If you're selling property in say, Australia, shouldn't you become familiar

Role-playing: If you screw up, screw up here

At the training sessions I organise, we have the participants divide themselves into four groups. For example, they might be the Eagles, Cockroaches, Lions and Snakes. The goal of each group is to develop a strategy (within five minutes) of convincing members from other groups to join it.

This forces participants to think creatively. What are the unique features of each animal? How will that feature bring tangible benefits?

Take an eagle, for example. The obvious features would be excellent eyesight and flight. But the participants learn to stress the benefits of those things. For instance, you can track the movement of your prey, and strike from above where they cannot defend themselves.

Don't limit role-play to company training sessions. It's great practice for tackling tough questions that put you on the spot, and a reminder that knowing the theory is not enough — you have to be able to deliver under pressure. Find the toughest friend you have outside of your client base, and have him or her throw you the biggest objections that the both of you can think of.

Make such informal sessions as realistic as possible. That means going to the same venues, wearing the same clothes and yes, having the same drinks as far as possible. Once you can consistently strike up a friendship, offer the right rewards and close the sale, you can focus on your demeanour, smile and posture.

All this will pay for itself as you learn to think on your feet in a safe, risk-free environment where the only thing at stake is your ego.

with what that neighbourhood, city and state has to offer? Imagine being asked, "Why should I buy something in Perth?" and not being able to answer! You'll need to be familiar with the neighbourhood, the restaurants, the nightlife, the recreation, the cool air and good climate — everything a resident instinctively knows.

More importantly, if the buyer wants to invest, what can you say about new developments, the competency of its management and the possibility of crime? If you're asked these questions, you'd better know the answers — or have a way of immediately finding out. Your customers are busy, and are unlikely to wait a day when they can find someone else who is more knowledgeable.

Between someone who knows the product *and* how it affects the customer, and someone who's only read the theory, guess who will be getting that commission?

Without good product knowledge, you're finished! There's no way you can convince anyone of the features and benefits if (1) you're not aware of them yourself, or (2) you can't communicate them in a way that convinces the customer of their value.

Conduct a client study

Most new clients will come via referral from existing ones, and be passed to you directly or through your mentors. Take this opportunity to conduct a client study; learn everything you can about the prospect's personality, likes or dislikes, including whatever they have said on Twitter, in their blogs or during interviews with the press. That can be as simple as Googling their name, followed by the word "interview". Don't discount the work of tabloid "paparazzi" either, because photos can give vital information about their preferred activities and stomping grounds.

Clients, and their support staff, like it when you know and can discuss their values, preferences and working styles. For instance, if they are religious and cite a close relationship with God as a factor in their businesses, we know that (a) they probably won't appreciate you swearing in front of them, (b) they may be attracted to the hotels, facilities and shopping in our casinos rather than the gambling itself and (c) they might respond well to family-friendly entertainment options.

Ramit Sethi calls this front-loading the work — doing more at the beginning so the end is much smoother.

Notice how selling comes WAY, WAY at the end of this process. In fact, we call this "front-loading the work," because if you do it correctly, you virtually guarantee your product will sell by the time you ever offer it.[22]

Exhaustive research also equips you with an advantage: It helps you cultivate the ability to think two or three steps ahead, anticipate questions and learn what deals you can make.

Remember that your prospects and clients are highly intelligent and want the best deal possible; so a careful study will reveal what they find important and what they do not. For instance, you will learn enough to quickly know where to meet them halfway — such as reducing the fee for the flight in, giving them credit for gambling or discounting food and drinks.

Here are the "vital statistics" you'll need to consider:

1. Business and family background

As we saw, business founders and those who worked their way up understand risk and how it works. Inheritors place a higher premium on the experience itself; how much they can enjoy themselves. This information is likely to come up in interviews, so take careful note of it.

Also, what are their business goals and hopes going forward? If he has spoken about (for instance) improving environmental sustainability, it helps to understand the efforts his company is making in that area.

2. Values

If a client mentions a core value or a unique outlook in an interview, think about how that value has been shown in your company and work, and how it's demonstrated by industry leaders. Don't be afraid to share articles, blog posts and advice with your client; he'll be impressed that you went out of your way to do so.

Many whales are turning to Twitter to air their thoughts, so if your prospect has a Twitter account, check there first for a great window into their thinking.

3. Age

At the same income level, younger clients are probably more aggressive gamblers than older ones. My guess is that they want to make a name for themselves, and show that they can win enough to buy what they want — luxury cars, homes and clothes — without relying on their parents' money. They also seek bigger, flashier experiences, like private jet travel or a gourmet dinner capped off with $10,000 bottles of wine. If they want to impress their girlfriends, so much the better!

Younger clients are also more likely to keep coming back to you, making them repeat prospects who will give you business for the foreseeable future. One of my customers, whom I'll call JC, first brought in only $300,000. But as his wealth increased, he was risking more than twice that on a single bet! Today, he brings us about $25 million each visit. As your customer's age and wealth increase, so will the proceeds he brings you.

4. Ethnicity and culture

People don't form their beliefs in isolation. Culture-wise, Indians and Jews generally don't gamble as much as Chinese or Westerners. Even among Europeans, I have noticed that darker-haired groups like Italians tend to gamble more, or are at least more open to the idea. (In fact, the very word *casino* comes from the Italian language.)

It might take a little more work to attract prospects from groups that don't gamble as much, but it's worth it. Note that there are always exceptions — so get to know your prospect both as an individual and as a member of a larger cultural group.

5. Dreams and aspirations

What do they want, in the short and long term? Is it to expand their business, acquire another, or simply increase social responsibility to the less fortunate? Other wants may include getting VIP access to a Formula One garage or having dinner with a celebrity. If your company has connections to make that dream a reality, why not do that?

6. Financial state

How much credit can you give him? Is he in danger of bankruptcy? All of this will give you a knowledge base you can draw from in your approach and negotiations.

Check the papers

Before customer meetings, it's a good habit to quickly scan the financial pages, especially for information relevant to the whale's company or industry. That way, you'll have an inroad and a ready-made topic to talk about.

Remember, there is no such thing as too much information. Whatever you learn at this stage is merely a jumping-off point for closer, more intimate conversations between you and the whale. Media exposure is part of their lives, so why not use that to your advantage?

What we've learnt

1. Know your product, and anticipate any questions that might arise. If necessary, role-play them with a friend.
2. Front-load the work through as much research as possible on the client himself, and your understanding of the groups that he or she is a member of. Use this knowledge to plan the discussion accordingly, so you're never stuck.
3. Use media, both traditional and social, as a research tool. There is no such thing as too much information.

9

Platform Marketing and Social Media

Social media is changing the way we communicate and the way we are perceived, both positively and negatively. Every time you post a photo, or update your status, you are contributing to your own digital footprint and personal brand.

— Amy Jo Martin

I've come to the realisation that money is a slut. Chase her and she'll coyly run from you; ignore her and focus on greatness, and she'll pop up at your door begging to come in.

In the same way, it's not about chasing after money; it's about creating a platform to reach the right niche and serving them with value they are willing to pay for. *Then* the money will come.

It's often been said that the biggest players don't provide goods and services, but rather give people the *avenues* they need to do so for themselves. Think Facebook, the largest content and social media site in the world (which doesn't create its own content), Uber (which doesn't own any cars) and Alibaba.com (which doesn't directly store and ship products).

How does that relate to the casino trade and serving the ultra-rich? First, we need to realise that technology has made it easier to connect with others than ever before, and we have a far easier time reaching our audience.

But what we do with that reach is up to us. Do we hard-sell? Do we reach out and gently persuade?

Technology also shortens the learning cycle. Through a quick outreach test, we can learn what kinds of posts attract readers (and what kind of readers they are), and adjust for another test in just a few hours. What originally took months and years for brick-and-mortar stores now takes far less time.

The key here is to build a platform where your audience can connect with each other or you. It's not to get them a sales message, but to add to your network of allies. It's more like a tease, inviting them to find out more.

Your online platform

Obviously, selling a casino is a very different prospect from selling clothes, shoes or handicrafts, so each marketing platform is used in a different way, if at all. Social media has its place, but our industry has sensitivities and legal limits that prevent social media from being our primary tool of outreach.

Whales want to have a good time, and they value their privacy. To that end, I aggressively avoid Facebook. It's too easy for misunderstandings to start — I don't want to be photographed with some other woman, and neither do my customers. I have heard of relationships being destroyed thanks to a photo innocently uploaded on Facebook; it allows tagging of photos, so users instantly know where the photograph was posted.

It's too easy to get tripped up. If a client photograph is put up without the proper context, the gossip media will have a field day. In fact, a fugitive who'd been on the run for seven years was once caught after he posted a photo of his dinner!

The same goes for YouTube, Instagram and Pinterest. The threat to our customers' privacy is too high.

I do have a professional profile on LinkedIn, where others can get in touch and find out my background. I don't use it for client outreach, because customers tend to work more with referrals and people they trust. LinkedIn is a way for people to do a client study on me, not the other way around.

One interesting case study is Twitter. Because tweets are forced to be shorter than 280 characters, they require thoughts and posts to be extremely short and pithy. Links and videos, therefore, are the name of the game.

As a result, it's how many whales, especially younger ones, communicate their values, needs and outlooks to the world. A Twitter feed study should be an important part of your prep work, and it's an added bonus if you actively engage their accounts, re-tweeting and replying to their posts. Even better — why not quote their tweets at your meetings for an instant boost in rapport?

As for blogging, it's a no-brainer. Many famous whales, including some your customers might look up to, blog their thoughts and advice. If your customer does so, that's a golden opportunity to explore his thinking, research his contacts and open up lines of conversation. If he has mentioned a thought leader he follows, chances are that person has a blog you can look up.

And if you have the inclination to blog yourself, go ahead — as long as you keep it professional, explore suitable topics and remain consistent.

I know that many people do have Facebook and other accounts, which they use to keep in touch with friends. There's certainly a place for you to have them, provided you follow these rules:

1. Privacy is king, and whales guard it jealously

In my industry, no one has ever got into trouble for posting too little. Even if your field does benefit from social media outreach, always take care not to reveal personal information or the day-to-day whereabouts of yourself and others. The exception is if your business does so as part of a wider strategy (which the casino business quite assuredly does not).

So when dealing with whales, use Facebook *only* to document your personal, strictly non-business life, and keep a clear wall of separation between business and personal matters. Even so, take as much care over revealing personal information and photos as you would business activities. Avoid tagging photos with the casino name; treat anything work-related as off-limits to Facebook. Your friends, and clientele, will thank you for it.

2. Keep it professional

Like many other unfortunate social media users, a young single mother named Kaitlyn Walls was fired from her workplace after a too-candid Facebook post. "I absolutely hate working at day care [...] I just hate being around a lot of kids," she wrote. She was set upon by an online mob, and her employers at the day care centre she worked at quickly fired her. "I was just venting," Walls claimed.[23]

Too many people have lost their jobs due to ill-considered posts that they thought were harmless jokes, only for the joke to be on them instead.[24] Not every such dismissal may be fair, but don't take that chance.

Bottom line: Think twice before hitting that "Post" button. Yes, that applies to "private" posts as well — it can still be screen-captured and spread just as easily as anything else.

It's becoming more and more common for employers and clients to Google your social media profiles, so take care what material you set as public. By definition, anyone can see it; so ensure that everything you post makes you look more capable and passionate, not less. (If you're really looking to post information, there's no shortage of helpful sales strategies and business tips out there to share with others.)

Be especially careful with issues close to people's hearts, such as religion and politics. It's also wise to stay away from controversial topics, and avoid joining online "mobs". As the Miranda line goes: "Anything you say can and will be used against you."

3. If in doubt, don't post it

As valuable as social media and email are, no message is worth damaging your credibility over. Many people have found their messages or posts going viral for all the wrong reasons, and fairly or not, that is a part of how you will be remembered for the rest of your life. As anti-bullying organisation Stand Strong puts it: "If you have to think about hitting send, don't hit send."[25]

What we've learnt

1. Social media can be an asset or a liability. Use it wisely, and remember it is not a replacement for deep in-person conversation.
2. Many thought leaders blog, or use Twitter. Check them out, and keep abreast of industry developments.
3. Tailor your use of social media platforms to your company, industry and objectives. Keep things professional, and when in doubt, don't post it.

PART FOUR
EXECUTE AND CLOSE

10
The Three-Meeting Rule

> The proper function of man is to live, not to exist. I
> shall not waste my days in trying to prolong them.
> I shall use my time.
>
> — Jack London

Whales don't like wasting time. Neither should you.

Too often, I've seen salespeople go for appointments and return with no closure. True, they find out a lot. "This one's son is really stubborn," they might say. Or "His wife is even more domineering than he is!"

"So when do you see him making a trip?" I ask.

The answer is just a blank look. "I have no idea, I didn't ask him."

Meetings don't conduct themselves — they need to be part of a wider strategy. I'm all for making friends with prospects, and waiting till later to close a sale. Every connection is important, but some are worth more than others and give a better return on investment.

So I need time to decide whether a prospect is worth this process or not, and to do that, I give myself a limit of three meetings. By the end of this three-meeting "wooing" process, I'll know whether he is a gambler himself, or if he has friends he can recommend to us. At that point, I'll have the knowledge I need to decide how much more time to spend with him.

No one likes to waste time — but of course, the customer is not going to be the one who calls a stop to things. He's enjoying food and entertainment at your expense, so why should he put an end to it?

As the woo-er, it's your job to manage the hunt. No one just rents a fishing boat and tries his luck — they research the best rods and bait to use, the best spots to wait and the best ways to pass the time till a bite shows up. Then they plan things out so that the actual trip itself goes smoothly.

You'll have done all the homework; now the meeting itself has to be planned to the best of your ability.

Just as the sales process is a negotiation with a beginning, middle and end, each meeting must be planned to:

- Learn more about the whale and his habits which you haven't been able to glean from your research. (Not many people admit to being gamblers online or to interviewers.)

- Create a bond of friendship and mutual trust between the whale and yourself, as well as his family.

- Shift the whale closer to saying yes. The more you
  plan and deliver correctly, the easier the negotiation
  itself will be.

It's true that no plan has ever survived contact with reality. But the best ones have a way of being very, very adaptable to the changing situation, because they've taken exactly that possibility into account.

Consider the Victoria's Secret example earlier. Notice that I created a want — the customer wants the tickets, and is willing to do something for me to get them. The question, however, still remains: *how much?* He will need to commit to a minimum check-in sum to qualify, say $2 million. We don't say "loss" or "risk", even if the concept is the same. To risk $2 million, he will reasonably have to turn over, say, $20 million.

When customers hear a figure like that, they'll try to bargain. "What about $10 million?" Once you've something the customer wants and is willing to work with you to get, you've reached the point of negotiation.

At this point, the customer is on your side. He truly *wants* to come, but now you have to commit to a number the company is willing to provide. The more he turns over, the better it is for the company, but the riskier it is for him. If he is unwilling to agree on something within the company's range, you need to do internal negotiation — that is, convincing your bosses that he is worth taking on despite the lower risk.

How do you do that? Dreams, once again. While the company has limited resources, it needs to keep taking on customers to survive. I might explain to my boss that this customer, should we take him on, has the potential to introduce others worth far more.

Numbers are your friend. Trace the prospect's network, learn who he is in touch with, and leverage that. If this sale is closed, imagine how much more that customer could bring in! You need to convince your boss that he is worth the airfare, the entertainment and yes, the Victoria's Secret tickets.

Show respect for others

I recently opened a treasury account with a well-known bank in Singapore. To make an initial deposit, I withdrew $500,000 in cash, put it in a bag and headed to a branch near my house. I was dressed very casually, and the sales representative who served me almost did not give me a second look.

"I want to open an account," I said, bag in hand. "Can you tell me about treasuries?"

He reacted with the enthusiasm of a pupil who'd just been given a horrible class assignment. As we spoke, there was no enthusiasm or any hint that he was anything but irritated to see me. Finally, I straight-up asked him, "Are you going to be managing my account?"

"No, I don't think so. I'll be handling higher-net-worth customers soon."

"Congratulations," I said dryly. "Just open an account for me as a convenience. It's just for my savings." With that,

I put the bag on the table and opened it to reveal the cash inside.

His eyes went wide. "Half a million in cash," I told him. "Did you think I didn't have any money when I came in?"

"No, no, no!" he protested. "We can sense when people like you have money."

Well, you sensed wrong, I thought. He began fawning over me and attending to my every request, but it was too little, too late. He volunteered to handle my account, and I let him — after all, for all his haughtiness there was little actual harm he could do.

But whatever training the bank had given him, it wasn't working. He clearly reserved his respect and basic courtesy for the very rich, and if I hadn't exposed him, someone else would have.

Regardless of who stands before you, it's imperative that you treat them with the respect and decency due a fellow human being. Everything may be a deal at day's end, but the relationship you cultivate with others will play a big part.

Remember, the very rich are observant people — and because they are used to receiving deference from others, they look to how you treat the people you encounter as a guide to the kind of person you are. This includes not only receptionists and associates, but other hired staff such as security guards or waiters.

The Way of the Hunter

Have you ever had a shop assistant or service representative promise you something, only to get back and say it isn't available? Of course you would be angry and upset, and you might consider never visiting that shop or using that service provider again.

It's the same in casino sales. When both you and the prospect are drunk, he is likely to begin making all sorts of requests, like free food and drinks, a free private flight in, or social escorts for themselves and their guests. It's too easy to give in and say, "Yeah, sure. No problem. Whatever you say — I'll do it for you."

Too often, Hunters forget that they are still representing a company with finite resources and abilities, so don't commit to those big things immediately. If you agree to something and have to walk it back, it's not only unprofessional — it reflects badly on the company and yourself. And it is your boss who has to clean up the mess, because the client needs to be kept satisfied. I've had to do that, and I make it very clear that their mistakes are not to be repeated.

My advice for these situations is:

1. Keep your head at all times

Know and keep to your limits; never commit to anything while not in full control of yourself. Whatever the setting, be it a fancy restaurant, a karaoke lounge, a pub or a private plane in flight, it's still a business negotiation. Prospective clients will take the most they can get away with, even if it feels like they are taking advantage of your goodwill and the company's resources (which may even exceed their own). That's one trait that got many of them rich in the first place!

You and the client can be good, even close, friends, but any business transaction needs you to look at the more rational side of things. Hunters need the savvy to understand *when* to say a polite no, and the emotional intelligence to understand *how* — without straining the relationship.

2. Listen to the client

The best salespeople build emotional connections by understanding what their customers want, then offering them options. If I'm looking for a flat-screen TV to mount on my wall, I don't need a salesman who immediately shows me the latest curved-screen monstrosity! The relationship you build is one of exploring the need together, not interrogating them or pushing the latest products. I'm much more likely to buy from a salesperson who considers my needs, budget and available space, and actually knows the ins and outs of TV technology.

It's up to you to draw this out of them. In any conversation, you should be actively listening to what they say, picking up hidden cues, uncovering thinking processes and identifying points of concern. Try paraphrasing what they say — and use your knowledge of their fields, their own words and what you learnt before to get into their heads and form good questions.

Take the time to get to know them as friends, *then* learn what they look for in a casino or entertainment setting. Is it to rediscover the risk and thrill of their younger, hungrier days? Is it to reward colleagues and associates with a few nights of shopping and fun? Each of those things will shape your conversation and recommendations, and if you can provide the client with what he needs most, you will have something incredibly precious — his friendship and gratitude.

3. Say no with grace

Rather than refusing outright, suggest something better from your knowledge. For instance, a client going to Australia might request expensive French wine. "Hey, you're in Australia right now," you could tell them. "It's a bit silly to drink French wine. Why don't you try some of the local produce where it's freshest?"

I've had clients who wanted many bottles of the most expensive wines, like the $45,000-per-bottle Domaine de la Romanée-Conti. If I can't meet that request, I might say something like, "You know, I think Romanée-Conti is fantastic. I've drunk it myself, but I've found something else out there that's just as good, if not better. Maybe DRC is too hyped up?" Then I follow with my recommendation.

I can recommend other wines from experience; the more you know, the more you have to draw on to make clients happy. (I make it a point *never* to mention the lower cost of my recommendation, or use the word "cheap" or "cheaper". It creates the wrong impression in the client.)

But the bottom line is that you represent a business, and the cost of what you settle on should always be in the back of your mind — assuming you keep your wits about you!

4. Be honest about what you can (and cannot) provide

Agree to what you can, negotiate on what you cannot, and promise to get back on requests above your authority level. There's no point promising something that you need approval from many other people to get done. Instead, project and promise more of what you *can* provide.

For instance, if the client is a foodie and you can arrange for attractive discounts, play up the F&B angle and fill his mind with the cuisines he'll get to enjoy — which will cost him less and less as he comes again and again. Leave the logistics (such as private jet flights) for later, when you take their requests to your bosses.

5. Project confidence and professionalism at all times

This should be a no-brainer, but pay extra attention to your appearance and demeanour, and carry yourself well. Because you will meet clients in every kind of environment, dress accordingly. If I'm meeting Mr W in his office, of course I'll wear a suit. He himself doesn't need to dress up, but you're disrespecting him if you show up in a polo shirt or anything more casual. The idea is that because you want something from him, you have a lower assumed status and should dress more formally. (I wish I didn't have to say this, but I do.)

It doesn't really matter what brand your suit is — well-fitted sets from Giordano or Zara beat poorly fitted ones from expensive brands like Armani or Louis Vuitton any day of the week. One quality of the ultra-rich is their attention to detail, so make sure everything is clean, from your suit jacket to your shoes. Project pride in yourself, regardless of the brands you're wearing.

On the other hand, if you're meeting Mr W at a golf course, that's a different story. Formal wear there stands out, so the name of the game is polo shirts and casual pants like everyone else. The key is to understand the setting, and dress and behave appropriately. Be prominent and even loud if you like, but you must still dress like you logically belong there.

Don't just hang on to the client. You might meet him at a company or family event, where his staff or family members will also be present. Strive to be professional with everyone you meet, and make a positive impact on them should they be connected to your client.

And above all, always be polite to their personal assistants or staff members. They are the guardians of your clients' time, and a bad impression on them can wreck a relationship you have spent weeks or months cultivating.

Ladies: Spend time with wives and daughters

For female representatives, you have an incredible opportunity men don't share. Consider the vast influence the women in a male client's life have over him — they might say, "Honey, I want to go to Melbourne for shopping. I love the weather there."

What do you think the client will say? "Of course, dear. Let's go." These women don't become the wives and companions of such powerful men for nothing!

Everyone should mingle well with a client's loved ones, but it's a great bonus for female representatives to bond well with wives, daughters and female associates. Men can't spend too much time doing that, due to the different ways the sexes are perceived.

Some of the most powerful women around have a very understated presence, but we miss them to our peril. I was once having a cigar with the chairman of a well-known banking company and chilling with his friends, enjoying the best food and drinks money could buy. Off to one side, his wife and daughter were hosting the women.

Just after I invited the entire group to wine, the chairman turned to the women's gathering. "Hey," he called out to one of them, who had been quietly reading a magazine the whole time. "Are we gonna get those good wines Marcus is talking about?"

"I'm not sure about the wines we're having tonight, but I'm sure they'll be quite okay," she said, and went back to her magazine. That was that. She had remained alert enough to answer his question right away, without committing to anything she wasn't sure of.

Yet all the time, she had been observing us, listening to everything we said. Notice, though — she did *not* commit to the wine itself (which she wasn't sure of), and yet communicated what she intended directly and firmly.

I could only stare in awe. That woman was the CEO of a prestigious US casino chain! She outranked me and most of the room by far, yet she associated with the other women and did not interrupt us. She's no shrinking violet; in the male-dominated casino world, what she says gets done. Yet she is one of the humblest people I know, and I respect her greatly for that.

Chase people, not money

There are two kinds of sales closures — the deal sale and the relationship sale.

A deal happens when both sides want something the other can provide. Customers want to know where and how they can have a good time; we want to know how we can deliver that.

We don't want clients so much as clients want to come to us! In fact, when I approach many whales they say, "Oh, I don't know anyone from your casino. I've always wanted to go there!"

When a deal is closed, three parties need to be convinced of the benefits. I must be clear that the customer is trustworthy, gambles and pays well; the customer must be clear that the casino can provide him and his loved ones with a good time; and the company must be convinced that the customer will provide it with revenue.

Deal selling is when the client is attracted by what you have to offer, be it a set of concert tickets, a gold-plated iPhone or something else. Something other than the relationship they have with you seals the deal, and the customer agrees to your terms.

The negotiations in a deal sale focus on creating the wow factor and creating conditions agreeable to everyone. Deal sales form the majority of closures — around 70 to 80 percent. Because everyone wants a deal.

On the other hand, relationship sales happen when we like working with someone so much, we take whatever they're selling because we know they'll do a good job. In a deal sale, customers buy a product or service for its benefit to themselves; in a relationship sale, they buy it for the sale's benefit to the seller.

Now I firmly believe that every closure should be a good deal. At the end of the day, is the new customer worth the money and resources we'll spend flying his party in, entertaining them and keeping them gambling?

But a good run of relationship sales is what makes the difference between a merely average salesman and a superstar. A close is a close, and believe me, your bosses will notice if you achieve 20 percent more closures than everyone else! It's what elevates you to the next level.

In fact, some whales look *only* at the relationship. Here's what I mean.

When patience pays off

One of my customers, whom I'll call Mr G, is a prominent billionaire and household name in Singapore. He's an old man with a long and illustrious history in gambling — he's been doing it for longer than I've been alive. Yet he's fully paid up and has never owed any casino a cent, nor has he ever asked for a discount or any special treatment.

You'd think such a customer would be easy to take up. Not at all! In fact, those who make a lot of requests are easier to work with, because you quickly see what satisfies them and gets them coming. It is the quiet ones who insist on taking things at their own pace and refuse to commit or even to express their preferences that fill us salespeople with great uncertainty.

I knew Mr G even before I entered casino sales, but we did not have anything resembling a relationship. So when it came time to invite him over, I went to size him up.

True to his nature, he said nothing upfront about what he wanted, and never asked for this or that. He happily had lunch with me many times, but he was someone who never wanted to owe favours — at every meal I had with him, he insisted on paying the bill!

How can you deal-sell someone who isn't interested in dealing? When I thought it time to reveal my work, he took it calmly. I tried asking: "What do you need to come over, Mr G? Can we work something out?"

"No, it's okay. I'll take what you give."

But I had no idea what he wanted, or how we could give him an experience he would truly enjoy! I tried offering him a serving of expensive Petrus wine, but he shrugged it off. "It's okay, I drink cheaper wines like Penfolds. I don't really appreciate these things — I actually prefer beer."

Now I was in trouble. I texted him: "Mr G, we have a special deal with Penfolds. We'll serve you a signature dinner with your name on three bottles of their platinum wine."

His reply came less than a minute later. "I prefer something else. Thanks!"

So I decided to back off from the sale. Notice that I remained genuine — I truly enjoyed spending time with him, and decided to just get to know him better.

Two years passed. He must have liked me, because we

had lunch almost every week! It helped that his office was in the same building as mine, just a couple of floors up. (In fact, as I write this I'm expecting Mr G to text me another invite.)

"Marcus," he finally said. "Let's take a trip to your casino."

"Sure, Mr G. What happened?"

"It's been a long time since my last visit. Let's go!"

How could I say no? "Is there anything I can do to make your experience better?" I asked.

Mr G waved me off. "No, it's fine. It's been fine since we first met. I know what I was looking for, and you hit it right on the nose. I don't need anything else!"

So we went. He gambled, lost big and won even bigger. We stayed for drinks, and it was a deliriously happy Mr G who shouted, "Marcus!" across the room.

"Yes boss?" I called back. "What's up?"

"You're okay, Marcus. You're okay!" he yelled, loudly enough for all his friends to hear! He must've feared we couldn't hear him, so he yelled it twice more.

I could only grin. You sly fellow, I thought. You took two years to size me up!

Sometimes there's no alternative to waiting. If it pays off, it pays off. If not, stay honest and sincere — or you'll quickly be found out. Whales get where they are by being able to read others well.

An interesting postscript: Mr G made a deal to return to the casino about four months later. But just before he was due to board a 9 am flight our way, there was a problem and the company plane could not make the trip in time.

"Can you shift Mr G to a 2 pm flight?" I was asked. "That's the earliest we can do." The casino offered him $50,000 as a gesture.

"Boss," I said. "We have a problem and can only fly at 2 pm. How about $50,000 for the inconvenience?"

Most people would have put up with that sum for a short delay, but not him. "You think $50,000 will move me to your 2pm flight?"

Something in his gaze told me that I had best not press the issue. "Forget what I said," I said. "Let's get you a 9 am flight some other way."

"Very good," he answered, and that was the end of the matter.

Some people can be enticed with money and gifts, and others cannot. Mr G's time couldn't be bought with money, and he went wherever and whenever he wanted. I didn't antagonise or argue, but realised he was a big enough player for us to make that accommodation.

To this day, I make myself available whenever he wants to come by and gamble, or just have lunch. How can I not, when he's such a good uncle and friend?

What we've learnt

1. Sales meetings should be held with an eye on the relationship, your own resources within the company and your own professional conduct.
2. Use the three-meeting rule as an initial guide. Plan out what needs to be accomplished at the end of each

meeting, so you can quickly decide whether to keep prospecting them or move on.

3. Meetings are a chance to learn more about what your customer truly wants, and what drives them. Come up with a reward, then plan out together how both of you can make their dream come true.

4. There can be deal sales, and relationship sales. All sales should be a good deal, but a strong relationship can often drive the sale all by itself.

11

When Things Change,
So Do You

You must be shapeless, formless, like water. When
you pour water in a cup, it becomes the cup. When
you pour water in a bottle, it becomes the bottle.
When you pour water in a teapot, it becomes the
teapot. Water can drip and it can crash. Become like
water, my friend.

— Bruce Lee[26]

Remember the three-meeting rule? It's a starting point,
and not set in stone. I didn't follow it with Mr G, and the
first time I tried selling him at my casino, it didn't work. It
was a similar story for Mr L — I knew I would have to gain
his trust and become his friend first, and sell him an experience after.

Everyone is different, and responds to different
approaches. The DISC framework (introduced in Chapter 8)
is a useful starting point, and your background research will

have revealed more information you can incorporate. In fact, once you start the very first meeting, you should already have a rough idea how to take the sale from beginning to end, using techniques from your repertoire to refine things as you go ahead.

But the basic structure is there: Learn as much as possible, size the customer up, make friends and then — only then — go in for the sale.

Size up a customer from the first meeting. From your interaction, think: Would it be better to make a gung-ho approach, or a soft one? How will you handle outsize requests — will it be a joking "Screw you, I can't do that" or a conciliatory "Hey, I'm sure we can work something out, I'm just doing my job". Don't be afraid to discuss the matter later, or walk away if the situation gets out of hand.

In fact, this very threat might snap some prospects to the reality of things. "I can't do anything more," you might say firmly. "This is the best I can do. Take it or leave it."

The foundational idea is that the sale cannot be forced. It's an agreement to have an experience that you and the customer make together, so take care to make the customer consider the benefits and the possibility of attaining his goals — not just you as a person.

Confidence: What you truly need

Many of us have an instinctive fear of those in authority over us — they are the social equivalent of the alpha male entering the den and holding court, receiving deference from everyone and dispensing favours and punishments as he sees fit.

But you don't have to fear whales, because in the end they are as human as you and me. They may have more money and resources, but that doesn't mean they're better or worse than you.

Instead, what you need is confidence. Be confident of yourself, your product and the space your bosses give you to work with. If you honestly feel that the customer is asking for more than you can offer, and you're not trying to screw him with a bad deal, stand firm and don't back down.

If you must enter internal negotiation with your bosses, so be it — provided the customer is someone who can truly bring revenue to the company, whether through his own gambling or that of others that he refers to you.

Every sale is a balancing act between what the customer wants, and what the company can provide. If a prospective customer wants more than we're prepared to give him, it becomes our job to justify closing the sale to the company. If you truly believe that the customer is worth it and will benefit the company's bottom line in the long run, you should do your best to convince your boss. Keep trying one angle after another.

First, work with the customer and find a compromise. Then work with your boss and get another compromise. Consider that the customer wants all the perks he can get, while the company looks at revenue, the bottom line and the cost of delivery.

Try your best to close every deal, but don't be afraid to

walk away. I'd much rather lose a bad deal than close it and lose more in the long run.

Price and pricelessness

I sell based on packaging, product differentiation and providing top-notch services to my customers. As such, I despise price wars and salespeople foolish enough to enter into them.

If a customer mentions that a competitor is offering something cheaper or with better perks, never take the bait. Instead, differentiate enough to show how your company will give the customer what he wants better than the competition.

Here's how I handle it. Suppose I offer a $20,000 offset, and the customer says, "Hey, this other company is offering me $30,000 off."

I'll answer, "Really? Wow, I want that deal too! Can I go with you?"

At this point, the customer usually hesitates. That's when I know he's, pardon the expression, not telling the whole truth.

But remember that they're human as well. How different is this from haggling over chicken and fish at the wet market? People will always shop around for the best deal.

Of course, they need their dignity intact. So I politely ask about the other offer, then smoothly continue with the benefits my own company provides. It might go like this: "Boss, I admit that's a better deal if you take it. But look, you'll still be in Singapore and have to go back to the same old grind after it's done. I'm offering you a holiday in Melbourne. You'll get to see sleet falling from the sky. You'll get to see the penguins at Phillip Island. Your grandson is going to be so happy! How much is his smile worth?"

Notice how subtly this works. I don't contradict the idea that a better price is being offered; instead I turn it towards the entire experience the customer will get, creating in his mind an image above and beyond what the competitor offers. Price is merely one factor in the entire discussion, and I want him to see that what he is getting will be worth so much more. Because he instinctively knows that happiness is priceless, I point out that he will be attaining it for both himself and his loved ones. Who can put a monetary value on that?

As a sales chameleon, you should speak on the customer's level. Many whales, especially earners, have relatively little education and pulled themselves up through sheer hard work. Their speech patterns and tastes will reflect this.

So speak their language. If the prospect uses a lot of dialect, do the same if you understand it — for Chinese customers, a knowledge of even basic Mandarin, Hokkien or Cantonese can work wonders. In your research, you should have prepared seen an example of their speech patterns and preferences, so mirror that as much as you can, and use terms that they understand.

A sales chameleon combines research, technique and company resources to truly get into the customer's head, make friends with him and finally close the sale.

It takes time and practice, so don't take it to heart if things go badly at first. As you improve, the process gets faster and smoother, and you spend less time on blind leads and wild goose chases.

Crisis after the deal

Your duty doesn't end with the handshake and the signing on the dotted line. In many ways, it's only just begun — you sold them on the experience, now you have to deliver on it! Basically, you segue from being hosted to being the host. Anything can still go wrong, but if you keep a cool head, work well with the staff and show concern for everyone, things should turn out well.

This is what the service team is trained for, so trust the professionals. It's like a movie with the company as the producers, you as the director and the service team as the set crew. They make the vision you've built with the big stars — that is, the customer and his associates — happen.

But crises can and do come, sometimes long afterwards. Some time ago, I had a customer who I had an amazing relationship with. He'd been a great gambler over the last few years, and I was always pleased to host him.

One day he told me, "You know what, Marcus? I have a bunch of friends to introduce to you. Let's bring them down sometime."

How could I — or my bosses — refuse referrals like that? "That's great! Show them in." We negotiated a deal, and since he was such a reliable customer, we included a large credit line for everyone. I didn't have the authority to approve that, but I recommended that my managers do so, and they did.

But then disaster struck. Out of the party of eight, six defaulted on their bills! The total shortfall came up to $20 million, and it fell to me to collect. The default was a significant loss for the company, but I tried my best to keep my cool.

How did I recover? First, I admitted my mistake — I had trusted this customer too much, and let his associates get away with a deal they did not merit. Regardless of who was to blame, I treated it as entirely my fault, and obeyed the company's directions to see him in China and try to collect.

Now I could have argued back, pointing the finger at my managers. "Hey, *you* approved the deal, not me." But how would that have solved the problem? Instead, I did everything in my power to make things right. To this day, I try my best to get the debt paid off whenever I see that customer.

The idea is to move as quickly as possible from "It's my fault" to "Let's do something". Which brings us to the second thing I did — to become a source of solutions. Everyone wants problems to be solved more than they want someone to blame. Even if I am the scapegoat, so be it. Provide solutions rather than point fingers — remember that however bad things get, you and your bosses are on the same side.

Finally, build a strong reputation that will weather any crisis. Just as 80 percent of the work is done even before you first sit down with the prospect, the long-term effects are entirely dependent on how your managers have come to see you. Are you a team player and problem-solver, or a whiner and problem-amplifier? Do you bring in the customers and keep them coming back, or keep coming up with reasons why not?

If you haven't earned that trust from your bosses, don't count on their help cleaning up your messes. Good work beforehand incentivises them to work alongside you, rather than consider how to limit the damage you've done.

That's how I get the freedom and resources I need to keep pulling in the sales, and the company trusts me to do well even if that debt is never repaid. "I'm only as good as you let me be," I effectively tell them. "If you want to fucking micro-manage me, don't be surprised at micro-results. But if you give me free rein and enough resources, I'll do the best job you've ever seen."

And then I do it, and so should you.

Trust is something you earn every day. Think of your daily decisions in terms of their effects on your long-term results, and focus on building a strong working relationship with your boss and subordinates. Ensure that when a crisis strikes, or you move on, everyone knows that your responsibilities are in good hands.

What we've learnt

1. No approach, not even my own three-meeting rule, is set in stone. Every interaction is different, so prepare well *and* be ready to adapt your script and plans.
2. Work with confidence and pride in yourself and your services. You're building a relationship and offering something they want, so act like it!
3. Understand that money and price are simply small parts of the package. If you differentiate well and offer something your customer truly wants, price matters very little.
4. Solve problems by pre-emptively building a good reputation, taking responsibility, admitting your mistakes and working to find solutions.

12

A Whole New World

By definition, you have to live until you die. Better to make that life as complete and enjoyable an experience as possible, in case death is shite, which I suspect it will be.

— Irvine Welsh, *Trainspotting*

In the opening of Marvel Studios' movie *Iron Man*, Tony Stark and his team are on a flight when a huge party he planned breaks out. Clowns emerge from the rear cabins, the attendants start stripping and exotic dancing, and everyone has a blast.

Unlike the rest of the movie, that's not so far from reality. Some time ago, a customer approached me for a boy's night out... and those were some *big* boys, with net worths like you wouldn't believe. I booked a private jet to fly them around, and that turned into not one, but *four* intoxicating nights. We criss-crossed the Australia-New Zealand route, partying like crazy — at nightclubs, on the way to the nightclubs and on the way back to the plane!

Some truly massive bills arrived every few hours, only to be signed off as if they were nothing. At the end of four days, everyone was so wasted that they had little memory of the trip and needed to rest for a week. "What the hell happened?" they kept asking each other. (Of course, being alert the whole time, *I* knew.)

But events like that are unusual treats, like being taken for ice cream as a child. It's far more likely for our deals to be negotiated in restaurants, cafes or nightclubs. On one occasion I was in a karaoke joint in Indonesia, where I was to meet a customer in one of the rooms. There was a main lounge with a TV, side bedrooms and a toilet. The place was set up so you could have an entirely self-contained party, with food, drinks, sex and entertainment all in one place!

A word on the vice trade

It's our policy never to deal directly with the vice trade — that is, prostitution and recreational substances. Ever. We draw the line at social escorts, but we can't afford to dirty our hands with sexual favours and substance abuse.

If customers want those things, however, they have ways of making it happen on their own. But be very clear to any clients who ask, that such "add-ons" to the customer experience are officially none of your business.

If you're not sure about where to draw the line, speak with your mentors, learn how they handle such situations and decide how to do so based on the company's rules and your own principles.

Sordid or wholesome, we can pull it off. I'm especially proud of a grand garden dinner we had in Macau, where we booked the entire Four Seasons hotel. We turned the whole lobby and the gardens into a grand ballroom, complete with a classical string quartet, performances and dancing. The dinner was eight courses of the finest Chinese food, like abalone and shark's fin. The attendees were a who's who of society, including film directors and actors whose names anyone would recognise.

Cars are a favourite of our customers, and we once held a Porsche drive where they (our customers, not the cars) were helicoptered directly from their hotels to the race track. We've also held Lamborghini drives down the Great Ocean Road, the scenic highway that links Melbourne to the picturesque seaside communities of Apollo Bay and Lorne, as well as tourist vistas like the rock formations known as the Twelve Apostles. As customers make the drive, we station people at rest areas to serve refreshments.

Those are just the events *we* organise. As I said before, if you're a whale, you get the event tickets you ask for anywhere our company has operations — I've arranged front-row and backstage tickets to the Australian Open tennis tournament, the Australian Formula One Grand Prix (held at Melbourne's Albert Park racetrack) and the Melbourne Cup horse races.

Here be dragons: Saying no to danger

> [Alice] had never forgotten that, if you drink much
> from a bottle marked "poison", it is almost certain
> to disagree with you, sooner or later.
> — Lewis Carroll, *Alice's Adventures in Wonderland*

Seen Disney's *The Little Mermaid*? The entire plot is driven by the mermaid Ariel's rapture at the human world, as represented by the ship belonging to Prince Eric and his crew. She begins watching Eric and his courtiers living in a world she knows she can never enter... unless she takes drastic action and makes a deal with Ursula the Sea Witch. But the cost of entering that world, as we all know, almost destroys her and puts everything she loves in terrible danger.

That's not so different from those of us from average backgrounds seeing more money than we'll ever make in our lives being spent in hours or minutes. I'm talking tens of millions of dollars going like it's nothing. "What am I working so hard for?" we start thinking. We become like Ariel, obsessively drawn to another world we can see but will probably never truly join.

Because sales teams deal directly with whales, we are effectively amphibians, adapting to their world for as long as we need to live in it. And it does come at a cost.

I'm not going to lie about what can happen at sales events, good or bad. The drinks will just keep coming, and if you're not committed to keeping your wits, trust me — you *will* break. Because the sums of money at stake are so damn high, the parties are on a scale you may never have imagined before. Too many salespeople get sucked into a life of partying and alcohol abuse, and before they know it, their habits destroy them. Many a career has started with great promise in a sales office, and ended in shambles in a rehab centre.

That's right. The world of the ultra-rich has its dangers, and having seen them first-hand, I want to both share the perks of my lifestyle and sound a friendly warning. Because we're in charge of allocating resources and perks for customers, I've heard of incidents where customers deliberately tried to ply their salespeople with drugs, drinks and sex, in the hope of squeezing a few extra perks out of them!

But it's still business, so avoid becoming addicted, always keep your head and never commit to anything while you're not fully in control. The same rules still apply: Agree with what you can, negotiate where necessary, and take what's beyond your authority higher up.

I was a heavy drinker for many years, and over the last few years I've realised my liver is pretty much shot. As I write I'm on detox — if I drink again right now, I risk liver cirrhosis and other serious health issues.

Which is a problem, given that at sales meetings, the customers have a vested interest in lowering your guard and making you agree to things you never would have were you still in control of yourself. I'm not lying when I say I face incredible pressure to hit the bottle again, but more than closing any sale, I want to see my children grow up and succeed in life on their own terms.

So I consciously have to avoid drinking at sales meetings. This presents a dilemma, because customers who drink a lot do it till they're passed out on the dinner table — then insist on singing karaoke or doing whatever they feel like. To stay healthy, respectable *and* sober takes some verbal judo.

Even before you enter the meeting, be very clear what your drinking limit is and make sure you don't go beyond that. Needless to say, avoid driving if you must drink more than a very small amount.

Then when you are invited, the trick is to announce the decision not to drink as part of your duty to your loved ones, not because of someone else's concerns. Don't say: "I can't drink because my wife told me not to." (Their reaction? "What a pussy.")

Instead say something like: "Sir, I can't drink as I'm on medication today. If I do, it will affect my health. I've got a 10-year-old son. I can't die young." Or: "I'm taking a break from alcohol, because my liver is screwed. Look at my face."

Another, even better response is to point the focus back on the customer and what he wants. You can remind him of the perks you're arranging, then say something like: "Boss, I know that when I drink I'm not fully in control. I want to help you and your friends get the best deal possible, so I need to be very, very professional, cool and persuasive. I need to be thinking clearly."

Now you've taken the attention off your own obedience to others and onto your ability to stay healthy and do your job. The customer then becomes your ally, not your adversary. It really works!

Stay calm and keep what the customer wants front and centre, so drinks you are offered don't get in the way of what you have to offer him. So remember — saying no is sometimes necessary, but it's how you put it that matters.

What we've learnt

1. Commit to keeping your wits about you. Staying aware and understanding the consequences of your promises is hard enough when you're sober.
2. Follow all company directives regarding vice, and don't become addicted yourself.
3. If you cannot drink or accept the client's hospitality, graciously decline by pointing to your responsibilities towards him, your health or your loved ones.

PART FIVE
MOVING ON UP

13

Focus on Yourself

> Generally speaking, investing in yourself is the best
> thing you can do. Anything that improves your own
> talents; nobody can tax it or take it away from you.
> — Warren Buffett

I still remember the day I drove up to my third company's
headquarters and casino in Sydney, Australia, and saw it for
the first time. "This place looks like a factory!" I remember
thinking to myself.

Not for the first time, I wondered what I had been thinking when I left. My first and second companies had me providing clients with a bespoke experience in a grand hotel
building, worthy of being the best in the Las Vegas Strip. If
you've been to icons like the Palms, the Luxor or the MGM
Grand, you'll know what I'm talking about. Customers who
went there genuinely felt (and were treated) like royalty. And
here I was, about to persuade them to accept so much less
than they were used to. I wondered if even the greatest of

casino hosts, if suddenly forced to work for a smaller and less ostentatious place, would be up to it.

That, I had to remind myself, was what I was there to find out. After all, this was still one of the largest casinos in the country — but what I found was a management culture I had to help rebuild before it could achieve its full potential.

This would be the ultimate test of the principles I've talked about in this book. It's one thing to attract clients to the best experiences possible, but what about one that was still up-and-coming, and that I needed their help to build together? It would need all my connections, passion and dedication, and some part of me longed for that kind of challenge again.

A challenge to myself

I won't say it hit me all at once. Ennui has a way of creeping up on you, and if you're not carefully looking out for new ways to excite and challenge yourself, you'll find yourself trapped year in and year out in the same role, doing the same things. I was making my company incredibly rich, but I wanted to see how much better I could do in charge of a larger, more responsible team.

In short, I wanted to test my ideas and willingness to work harder and smarter. After all, didn't I believe there were no bad products — only bad salesmen? The last year I worked there I was dragging my feet to the office, a sure sign I had grown beyond what the company could offer. There were no available positions higher up, so I made the move to a new company that gave me better advancement opportunities. I'd been challenging my small team, and it was now time to challenge myself.

In short, I wanted to keep adding to my value. The old adage is true — you're paid not based on how hard you work, but how difficult you are to replace. The more experience and wisdom you gain, the more you bring to your employer. That means the more you justify your presence within the company and among your clients, and the more you're worth to them, the riskier the decisions you can be entrusted with. Your salary is simply a reflection of this.

I'm not putting junior marketers or janitors down by saying this, but the truth is that as vital as their services are, they're so easily replaceable that each one isn't paid as much as, say, a doctor or lawyer who provides a far more valuable service, and has become qualified to do so after many years of difficult training. After all, which would you pick if you could only receive help for one: your health and professional reputation, or the cleanliness of your workplace?

"Give me an opportunity," I told the group CEO trying to recruit me. So I was made a Senior Vice President of international business (a much better job title than I'd had before, and I quickly rose to become President), and put into a regional role. Sales around Southeast Asia were now my responsibility, and team leaders of Singapore, Indonesia, Malaysia, Thailand, the Philippines and other parts of the region were under my watch. That amounted to some 30 percent of the company's revenue.

What attitude should you take towards team leadership, when it's suddenly not just you bringing in the numbers, but others as well? What if your success depends on your ability to put in the work, *and* motivate others to do the same?

There's no point having the best principles in the world without the resolve to do the right thing by them — after all, in that case they're nothing more than suggestions!

That was how I found myself expanding our business throughout Southeast Asia, and making inroads into China and Macau. Was I stepping on my colleagues' territory? Certainly. But I knew that other team members of all levels had my back, because I had a track record of cold, hard earnings to back me up. Within the first year of my taking the position, business had grown by 67 percent!

Many of my clients before had come from those same areas, making it far more important that they helped me out — and because of our great relationship, most did. While numbers can be inflated in the short term by bringing in bad credit clients (that is, those who don't pay the debts they owe us), that certainly wasn't the case here.

It's the same with great marketers, and the destiny I want for you and myself — to be worth so much that companies compete for our services, not the other way around!

I went to work with the techniques I've shown you, while disseminating them to my team and staying accountable for their performance. I'm not saying this to brag, but merely to show how effective they are. Whether they liked me personally or not, we had cold, hard proof no one could argue with.

When I arrived, my team comprised just eight people,

which gradually grew to some 30 as our operations expanded. My job was simply to bring the best out of all of them. When I ran the sales numbers at orientation, I got a sense of what their "just okay" standard was. (Standards aren't necessarily transferable between companies, but you do need to set reasonable targets.)

My aim, and I hope it's yours too, was to achieve above and beyond what was expected. I hope if you've got this far into the book, you'll agree that hitting the minimum standard required isn't enough.

There are several factors to be held in balance, and it's up to you to decide which applies in any given situation. I talked earlier about understanding and managing your boss' expectations, but promotion means your subordinates will also be affected by what you do — after all, that's what leadership means.

Too many great doers are expected to become leaders, despite the skill set often being entirely different. Their eventual failure is known in management training as the Peter Principle, after the Canadian academic Laurence J. Peter, who first outlined it like this:

> In a hierarchy every employee tends to rise to his level of incompetence. ... In time, every post tends to be occupied by an employee who is incompetent to carry out its duties.

One observation from former US Navy SEAL Jocko Willink's podcast holds an important truth: a weak leader above you is actually a great opportunity to lead both yourself and your teammates.[27] Perhaps one of the most important skills leaders of any level can have is the ability to take advantage of any situation, good or bad.

Having a strong, motivating leader (a rare occurrence for me) is of course a great thing, but a weak one may not be the disadvantage many think it is. Rather, he or she provides a chance for you to step up. My new leaders made me own many tough decisions early on. They demurred too often and kept the status quo, despite the fact that they had capable people working for them.

All signs pointed to the company being able to do much better, and I wondered if changing things up, removing dead wood and incentivising top performers would work better. If my managers had no interest in finding out... well, I would.

Doing beats liking

Despite my having been talent-scouted, I still had to win over people who had never heard of me or worse, saw my entry as a threat to their own prospects. I would have to be so successful that whether they liked me personally or not, they would need to work with me to secure their own success. As I said before, friendship is good and even desirable, but both sides still need to tangibly benefit.

Here are the principles that, on reflection, enabled the sales lessons I've talked about to scale up to the small team, division and company level:

1. Ownership and accountability

Team leadership is about achieving the best results possible from your team, by empowering them, taking responsibility for their training and growth, and ensuring they have good targets to meet. Whatever problems come up, you own your team's response to them. In the same way that I examined different kinds of whales before, you must examine various circumstances and empower your team to work through them.

This means you have to constantly work with your teammates to identify both the good and bad, open up communication with them to ensure they trust you with any result, and set the right example for them. I said before never to let the words "I don't know" cross your lips before customers — now you must do the same before your subordinates and bosses. When we see people who blame others (even if they themselves aren't in the wrong), we rightly think of them as the sort of person who throws others under the bus.

I've had too many bosses who set negative examples, and I myself have occasionally failed to live up to those high standards over the years. But which is better — having high standards and sometimes failing to meet them, or having low ones and meeting them every time?

2. 360-degree management

It's one thing to achieve sales results and impress clients on your own, but another to do it while being watched by superiors and subordinates alike. In effect, you'll be managing your bosses, your same-level peers *and* your team members. Getting the best out of your team involves aligning their expectations and goals with your own, and working with them on planning and execution.

Of course, it's difficult enough doing it with colleagues you like and can work well with; but what if you can't stand each other? I had my share of such leaders in my new company, but the techniques I'll show you work regardless of your existing relationship.

Getting along as friends helps, but it shouldn't be a make-or-break factor. Apply these techniques, and there's no reason you won't be able to work towards your common goals, regardless of your personal differences.

3. Set up the fundamentals so succession is smooth

If the entirety of your team's success depends on a single person or a small group, it's like balancing a pyramid on its point. You won't be in that position forever, and if you aren't building your unit up to outlast you, it was never your team or company you were building in the first place.

It's said that leaders need to work themselves out of a job, and that means egotism has no place here. Your personal pride can be in the car, and indeed it can warn you of many a bad situation or person; where it should not be is in the driver's seat.

4. Seize every opportunity to be there for your team

For instance, even if I can't be in the office, there's nothing preventing me from checking in on them (and my clients) via tools like Zoom or LinkedIn. I've even gone the extra step and written testimonials for team members I couldn't keep despite my best efforts.

The principle here is simple: I treat people the way I would want to be treated, and with so many tools available to help you along, there's no excuse not to go the extra mile for them. After all, it may be me who needs their help someday, and a well-tended relationship is like a "bank" of goodwill we can draw from, over and over again — to the benefit of all of us.

"Exemplary leaders bring out the best in others," note James Kouzes, Barry Posner and Deb Calvert in their book *Stop Selling and Start Leading*:

> The expectations you hold as a leader provide the framework into which buyers and internal partners fit their realities. Your positive expectations shape the way you behave toward others and how they engage in their work.[28]

A disruptive pandemic like COVID-19 should be a mirror that reveals the faults in your leadership, and warns you to deal with them quickly. Bad times don't create them, but rather expose them to the light. As the saying goes:

> Good times create weak people.
> Weak people create bad times.
> Bad times create strong people.
> Strong people create good times.

It's an over-simplified axiom, but in a complex world, those who can create simplicity in the right places (and help others see it) can light the way. The days of "I pay you to do your job and not involve me" are over.

What we've learnt

1. Invest in yourself and look for new challenges to grow your skills and value.
2. See less-than-satisfactory leaders as an opportunity, not an obstacle.
3. Take ownership of everything that happens with your team, while guiding and empowering them to solve problems without you.
4. Treat others the way you want to be treated, and go the extra mile for them.
5. Crises don't create faults; they reveal them.

14

Service Recovery
or Bust!

Nobody goes to that restaurant any more. It's too
crowded.

— Yogi Berra

Despite your best efforts, it's finally happened. You're just
one person, and your teammates can't be everywhere and
do everything at once. Whatever the case, the ball's been
dropped and one of your top clients has walked away. And
you don't know why.

In a world where your competitors want you for lunch,
you can't afford to have him going to them. It's even given
me something of a split personality — on one occasion, one
client missed my previous company so badly, he wound up
leaving my present one for a game there. I was competing
not only against them, but my past self as well!

In the earlier chapter on solving problems as a good
host, I mentioned what happens within the establishment

itself that you can see and is within your control. That's rescuing the situation, but service recovery happens a few hours, weeks or months later, depending on when you find out about the problem and why the client hasn't returned. After all, if you have bad service or don't like the food at a particular restaurant, how likely are you to actually complain instead of leaving and never coming back?

If you're lucky, the customer may ask to speak to a manager, but "few dissatisfied customers actually ask for a superior," notes Ross Cranwell at Stella Connect. "Most will simply move on to another brand, and never do business with you again."[29]

That has actually happened to me, and whenever possible, I follow the Golden Rule. I treat places where I don't like the food or service the way I want my company to be treated — that is, I tell them why on the spot. Once, I was having collagen soup at one of my favourite hotpot restaurants and I realised it tasted funny. Another course of prawns came, but when I bit into them I found them too powdery, a sign that they weren't fresh. What a disappointment after three months without hotpot!

We were asked for our feedback (a good practice) but what the restaurant did after we gave it cost it our patronage. "We gave your feedback to the chef," the Support Manager told us later. "He said they were fresh prawns!"

"I'm telling you what I think because I care about your establishment," I said. "If you don't want that privilege, I'll take it elsewhere." And I did.

Recovery done right

Service recovery has a crucial Step Zero, and done well, it makes the rest of the process much easier. This is to build a general culture of encouraging feedback, so that the issue the customer has can be dealt with immediately. Wait too long, and the customer will probably have forgotten the specific slight... but you bet they will remember how it made them feel.

It could just be the occasional reminder to "Let me know if you need anything" or "Don't hesitate to call me for anything you need". It doesn't need to be too frequent, but your guests will respond much better once they know your services are available at any time.

One good practice is service empowerment, and its most famous incarnation is at the Ritz-Carlton hotel chain. "Each Lady & Gentleman at The Ritz-Carlton, at all levels, are [sic] empowered to spend up to $2000 per guest, per incident," says the hotel's Leadership Center.

It doesn't always need to be so expensive, and indeed this discretionary power is very rarely used to its full extent. But team members know they don't have to go through multiple levels of management for approval, and it shows trust in them to do the right thing and solve problems in a self-initiated, creative way.[30]

Respect for the customer cannot be feigned, and because (as I've said before) the guest experience is something they, you and your company create together, you have to take the lead in encouraging friendly, open dialogue. This is where your friendship pays for itself, because the guest will be far more open and honest with you. This will be the case even for Singaporeans or members of certain cultures who are less likely to give any sort of feedback.

And if it's an issue you can resolve immediately, you'll have shown yourself to be both trustworthy and empowered to help him or her out. Who doesn't want a capable staff member in their corner?

But if it can't be immediately taken care of or you only find out a long time afterward, don't fret — even if the complaint is put up on social media for the world to see. Stay calm and move to Step One — which is to draw honest, constructive feedback out. You might say something like: "Boss, we're very thankful you decided to join us. Is there any way we could have made your experience better?"

Have a team member (ideally, the marketer who worked with the guest) call him back and gently raise the question — or even better, arrange a face-to-face meeting. The guest must have the impression that we're there to help correct the problem so we can help him have a better experience next time. His feedback, we must assure him, is a crucial part of this.

One means of purposefully rebuilding the connection is to connect one avenue closer than the original criticism. If it came by email, social media or an online feedback form, call the client back; if it came through a telephone call, use the follow-up to arrange coffee or some way to meet face to face.

Step Two is to apologise, acknowledge the problem and take ownership of any problems. People hate it when staff members dismiss their experiences, defend their business, or worse, throw the blame back on them. If a restaurant waiter gets my order wrong and I point it out, the very worst thing they can say is, "But I heard you order that item, not the one you're pointing at!"

Instead, acknowledge the issue and assure the customer that you will do what it takes to satisfy them. It's usually the case that a sincere "We're truly sorry for the error" placates them and opens the door for their return.

It's been my experience that when the right opportunity comes along, they'll remember you and give you another chance. For instance, if it's their wedding anniversary, their birthday or some other significant event, they'll probably think of you — and if you've structured your offer well, your chances of getting them back are good.

Step Three is to reward the customer. In our industry, it could be an additional perk, more credit or a free bottle of wine. By doing this, we're acknowledging the inconvenience they've gone through, and assuring them that we'll make things better next time.

In Step Four (and this is where your entire team must come together), review common problems and identify systemic issues that cause them in the first place. Do more complaints come from booking, room maintenance, the casino floor itself, or someplace else? Has someone committed above their level and been unable to deliver the goods? Where else has the customer's journey from prospect to guest been made more difficult than it should have been?

The power of empowerment

Don't underestimate the power of having an empowered team member assure the customer that they'll make it right, and then take the necessary (but now much easier) actions needed to do so. One of my richest, most powerful clients, Mr B, drove that message home at my birthday dinner event.

I was preparing for the event and dressed up to the nines (complete with bow tie) when the distress button in the gambling hall was pressed. I arrived to a most fearsome sight. The entire hall had been trashed, with cards ripped to shreds and tables and chairs knocked over. Mr B had clearly brought his infamous temper along, and there was no avoiding it.

He immediately laid into me, complaining that our service and gaming teams had been too slow in rolling over the chips and running new games. According to him, our negligence had cost him $50 million!

The only thing to do was let him vent, take note of his frustrations, and own the mistake so he was assured I would do my best to fix it. When I could get a word in, I took full responsibility rather than push the blame to anyone else.

I acknowledged our error that we had understaffed his room, and we should have anticipated his needs and assigned more team members to serve him. I gave him a sincere apology and promised to make it right; there was nothing I could do immediately, but I would do my best to resolve the situation amicably.

Owning the mistake may have seemed risky, but it was the right thing to do and I tried not to let the terror I felt show on my face. What if the company didn't back me up, and he decided to come after me? What if he showed up at my event and trashed the place in front of everyone else?

Eventually his steam ran out. I pledged to honour my words and make the situation right, and he let me return to my dinner preparations. The phone call I had been dreading came not long afterwards — Mr B would be joining us!

Fortunately, my ownership of the situation before had indeed calmed him down, and when he came, he was all smiles. Halfway through the event, he motioned me over and asked me for a cigarette. "Hey fat boy, you know what it's like when you lose a lot of money," he said. That was the closest I got to an apology, but did I feel better after that!

Words are one thing, but as we've seen, no one becomes my client without being my trusted friend first. That honour between us was what paved the way for the service recovery that followed.

Make sure you have clear facts on your side, and your team members are trusted to deliver them. This should be a regular exercise, and each service recovery will show you blind spots and what you need to improve. That's how your team can grow, with the confidence that the same mistake will not be made twice.

What we've learnt

1. Service recovery must be part of a constant process of customer engagement and drawing out, listening to and acting on feedback.
2. Empower team members to deal with problems immediately as needed, so only what is escalated to you needs to be personally dealt with.
3. Be grateful for the feedback and don't get defensive. The relationship is more important than your ego.
4. Be on the lookout for systemic issues, so you can resolve them before they become more serious problems and begin driving guests away.

15

Everyone Is Needed

I got a safety violation for trying to shoot live rounds downrange and attempting to look around at the same time. Guess what? You can't do both. [...] A leader's job is making the call as the command and control for the team. If you're not doing it, nobody is doing it.

— Leif Babin, former SEAL officer[31]

It's a common problem in the military and civilian worlds alike — leaders breaking down trying to do too many things at once. Add the pressure of meeting the numbers or coming under enemy fire, and it's very easy for everything to fall apart.

Team management means taking responsibility for your team's willingness and ability to do the work. It's one thing to work overtime yourself, but quite another to expect others to do so alongside you willingly. I don't need to tell you that past a point, it won't help if you're the only one doing it!

I'm not for one moment suggesting that you and your

superiors must like each other for these to work — in fact, for much of my career I've had bosses who, to put it diplomatically, preferred my results to my presence. Indeed, promotion means you'll have to draw the best from all kinds of people, many of whom will not gel with you personally.

That was the case at the new company, where my subordinates were initially cold. One of them was an industry veteran far more experienced than I was, who resented the fact that I had been "parachuted" in as *his* boss! To him, I was blocking his advancement within the company, and it galled him to be reporting to someone younger and less seasoned than he was.

Here are the qualities your team should have, or try to acquire:

1. Commitment to the company and its goals

It's human to slacken after a high, but it can be taken too far. At the end of fiscal year 2019, we let the previous year's praise go to our heads and actually *failed* to achieve our target numbers. We were approaching the end of the year, and would have been in serious trouble if we didn't turn things around quickly.

I'd like to say I stayed in control and made the right decisions with a cool head, but looking back, panic, self-doubt and depression got the better of me. I was so paralysed with fear that I had let my team, my bosses and most importantly, myself down that I lost all interest in my work.

I didn't get the support I needed from higher up, and that made things even worse. The burnout was clear to my team, and they knew what they had to do — they would have to find a way to close the gap, with or without me. They assured me that they would carry me through and figure out how to do this, and I saw their commitment take a tangible form that saw us starting fiscal year 2020 strong. Their strategies worked, bringing us the "cushion" we needed for the new year. COVID-19 hit us badly, but that eleventh-hour effort gave us a buffer in the storm.

Whether any team member likes me personally or not is immaterial. Their loyalty must be to the team, and that is front and centre in how I recruit. When it's time to get down to work, I want to be joined only by those who are already all in. Anything less is dead weight, and those people are better off working elsewhere.

I ensure no one is asked to do something I will not do myself. If I need someone at 3 am for something important, I expect them to be available — but also ensure they're rewarded well for the effort that's asked of them. It's not something you can ask of others lightly, and it can only come from having a close working relationship with them.

Perhaps no one is more instrumental to "gluing" us together than my assistant and strategic planner. Where I am passionate and hot-headed, she is cool and diplomatic; where I might carelessly lose someone's loyalty or support, she's there to restore it, or smooth the person's departure if they truly aren't a good fit.

One of the most important steps to commitment is ensuring that as far as possible, our individual strengths are amplified, and our weaknesses covered for.

2. Clarity of leadership

I know it sounds redundant, but the term "clarity" here refers to everyone being on board with what we're aiming to do, and actively maintaining a culture that enables us to work as a team towards it.

This means that even before anything is asked of them, I want my team to be clear about their goals in the short, medium and long term. Leaders at all levels must be aware of their responsibilities and goals, and how every role fulfils the intent of the entire company. They must know what military planners call the Commander's Intent — the ultimate goal of the mission.

"Junior leaders must be empowered to make decisions on key tasks necessary to accomplish that mission in the most effective and efficient manner possible," note Willink and Babin. "Every tactical-level team leader must understand not just what to do but why they are doing it."[32]

By knowing the entire framework and the reasons behind each part, and the limits of their decision-making authority, they're free to create their own subordinate plans and take ownership of them. It may work for someone who resents that you're in charge of them, by putting their destiny and need to make the numbers into their hands.

The previous parts of this book were simply tools and sample plans on how to use them. Because nothing is set in stone, encourage your subordinates to adapt these approaches and create new ones suited to their personalities and expertise. Because they have come up with those plans themselves, I know their commitment to them (and the whole team) is unquestionable. This must be the case, whether I'm managing one person or several hundred.

3. Adaptability to new circumstances

My decision to leave a glitzy, established gaming company for another, up-and-coming one (twice!) was effectively a test of my ability to adapt, and of whether what I had learnt and the relationships I had built could do the same.

It's a well-worn cliché that no battle plan survives contact with the enemy, and so our strategies and methods need to be two things — comprehensive enough to plan for such problems, and simple enough to be quickly and easily executed. We have to be able to change the plan as needed, while maintaining the same vision and end goal.

Go one way, and you risk problems in coordinating and communicating clearly, with team members trying to do too many things at once; go the other, and they'll be caught flat-footed and forced to think on the fly. With so much at stake, the former situation risks devolving into chaos, while the latter is a gamble at best, with odds no casino-goer would want to play with.

Priorities, needs and goals can rapidly change, and seeing this is what your efforts should focus on — actually finding clients might need to take a backseat as you work with your team to build situational awareness and change tactics as needed. If anything, the COVID-19 pandemic has been a brutal test of entire industries' ability to do exactly this.

Generational change

One interesting observation I've made over the years is how different generations of great entrepreneurs have approached the uncertainty of business. In the past, when communication and information transfer weren't as instant as they are today, leaders had plans for every eventuality they could think of. Everything was discussed, codified and written out, detailing what to change and how. Those plans were taken out and reviewed before anything was done. A new idea wasn't even pursued until venture capital could be raised and it was tested over and over again by focus groups.

The opposite is true today of the new startups coming out of the gates. Because new entities can be created and markets all over the world entered so quickly, business ideas and their refinement can be iterated, changed and tried over and over again.

There's little use for the planning and slow, incremental change of the past — instead, entrepreneurs learn by doing, refining their products and services, and iterating until they have it right. If the whales you're meeting with like this conversation topic, by all means bring it up!

Either way, mistakes will be made. Jeff Bezos is the richest man *because* he's made hundreds of mistakes, and will make hundreds more. What he does well is make the most out of successes, reduce the fallout from those mistakes, and quickly drop ideas that are bound to spiral into failure. That adaptability is how risks are managed and investors kept on board.

Adaptation can require painful change, something many companies are either too willing or not willing enough to carry out. If it involves recklessly removing people or restructuring entirely without managing the entire process and understanding why each action needs to be taken, you've given up great talent and capability for little gain. If you're not aggressive enough to make those changes, like companies with great reluctance to dismiss anyone or change anything, the required changes will never be made!

Even worse are those companies that actually realise this, but aren't forthright in easing unneeded employees out the door, or aren't willing to pay their severance package. Instead, they create such difficult conditions that those employees are forced to resign on their own. It's a despicable way of lowering headcount and restructuring, but those companies and whoever works for them deserve each other.

Like me, my circle of customers had to make the switch. My third company was less "swanky" than my second, but as my friends, my customers would definitely be willing to listen if I helped them see its strengths. Sydney is a beautiful city with incredible weather, great food and bracing blue skies, and our service would be second to none. Because we had moved from deal sales to relationship sales (see Chapter Ten), they were happy to take my word for it and join me in building new and compelling experiences for them. And our team was there to ensure they loved every minute of it.

That kind of dedication in a team cannot be replaced with any amount of glitz or glamour, and our teams worked so well together that despite the humbler facilities, my third company actually pulled ahead of my second, and consistently held that position!

That brings me to the next point: the trust that keeps staff members happy and focused despite any problems they have, so they focus on our common goal of keeping our customers happy.

4. Trust at all levels

Leaders of all levels need to trust each other so that they will execute their tasks and keep you and each other informed as needed. That way, you'll only need to directly work with and manage those leaders immediately below you. And because you trust one another, you'll be able to sound out tough decisions and encourage everyone to bring up their points of view.

I don't need to ask if you can do your job; I know it's in safe hands, and if you don't have a way at the moment, you'll make one. Trust must be well established, observes Willink in his book *Leadership Strategy and Tactics*, "because there are times when the only thing holding a team together up and down the chain of command is trust".[33]

In a dynamic, fast-changing situation where we have no choice but to order one another around (and in the casino world, such problems are common), everyone must know it is not the time to ask questions — just execute and get the job done. Because we trust each other and know we're open to one another's concerns, our relationship allows us to cooperate with and correct one another on the fly. If our subordinates can't carry an instruction out, "I have to trust that he's seen something that I don't see," says Willink. "I have to trust that he would do everything to carry out my order if he could — but he can't."

My bosses were often reluctant to make the tough decisions, but they placed enough trust in me to give me a relatively free hand to run the company's sales and marketing arm. I'll share more about managing them in the next chapter, but for now it's enough to note that this was because I ensured my efforts supported them — in effect, helping all of us look good.

I balanced the time spent looking at the big picture with getting to know my team and walking the ground with them. As each member developed his own style and method of befriending and working with clients, I took the time needed to help them refine their presentation and person-reading abilities, through the very techniques you've already read about.

I'm particularly proud of two of my protégés, whom I hired from my second company to join me at my third. I sensed that they had that fire in them and could be groomed to become incredibly successful hosts and marketers. By that time, they already had several years of experience each. There was no point forcing my instruction on team members before they had a sense of what they did and didn't know.

I gave them the limitations of what they could commit to, and turned them loose on the customers on their contact lists. They didn't even need to come to the office or update me regularly, as long as they got the closes I expected

— after all, there's no point having a large database if you can't turn its entries into loyal customers.

After three months, they came back with results that could certainly use improvement, and asked for my help. Now that they were more "down to earth" and open to instruction, I taught them the techniques I shared earlier, helped match them with customers they were compatible with, and guided them on their presentation and other "soft" skills. Today, they're successful senior sales executives in their own right, and I couldn't be prouder of them.

No big or repeat customer can come through our doors without us having built a comprehensive profile of his businesses, spouse and children, partners and associates, personality traits and preferences. *Then* we match what we have to offer with what each member will like, presented by a team member who can best sell it — so an entire package can be customised for them.

It's part and parcel of working as a team, both internally among colleagues, and externally with clients and friends.

Notice how the same principle applies here — genuine connection and friendship cannot be forced. They must, however, be aims to work towards, and that includes establishing inroads into the work, life and interests of team members and customers alike.

Loyal repeat customers and ambassadors

The measure of our success isn't just the money. As we've seen, gambling revenue is simply a reflection of the loyalty our customers feel, one that draws them back to us again and again. They don't stop at spending their money with us; ideally, with these techniques you'll turn them into ambassadors, ready to send their friends and contacts our way for the time of their lives.

There have been many incidents where my inexperience or political infighting resulted in plans going awry and me becoming a flustered mess — yet surprisingly enough, some customers even stepped up to help. If anything, it shows that once you've got the wheels turning and building those friendships, these whales effectively become your partners and cheerleaders, precisely because they trust you to do your best for them. *That* should be the aim that each team member, from sales to the C-suite to the hospitality and support group, should have in mind.

At every level, you can be a leader. I wish you all the best in becoming the one that Steven Pressfield says:

> ... defines the cause for which the warrior offers sacrifice. Nor is this dumb obedience, as of a beast or a slave, but the knowing heart's pursuit of vision and significance. The greatest commanders never issue orders. Rather, they compel by their own acts and virtue the emulation of those they command. The great champions throw leadership back on you. They make you answer: Who am I? What do I seek? What is the meaning of my existence in this life?[34]

What we've learnt

1. Get the right people, and get them on board with your plans and purposes. No one is above learning from their subordinates.
2. Empower subordinates to make their own plans and take action — within the limits set by higher management and in line with their goals.
3. Be open to change, and adapt your plans as needed. COVID-19 will not be the last major shock to your industry, and the lessons you learn here must be carried forward.
4. Leaders need to trust each other, and a well-run team will have clear areas of responsibility in line with everyone's strengths and weaknesses.

16

Managing Your Bosses

I learned to subordinate my ego to the mission and to my boss. Does that mean I am weak? No, it means I put the team and the mission above myself so that we can win.

— Jocko Willink[35]

I've shared earlier how I got my bosses on my side, and got the freedom to run things my way as long as I got the results they wanted. Now it's time to share a touching incident of how my team managed *me*.

My birthday falls on 18 August, historically a low point in the year as no major international public holidays fall during this time. It's supposedly a lull period, but my job as a sales leader was to ensure there was no such thing as a lull period.

I got the idea of setting up a birthday celebration for myself, and my title of President allowed me to name it the President's Invite. It would be a prestigious event for my best VIP friends, with the intention of having them gamble after dinner. I wanted it to outlast me, which was why I did not bill it as my own birthday party.

That didn't stop me from getting cold feet, and I fretted about the message I was sending — who was I to invite my ultra-rich friends and claim a status like that? Who was I to expect them to take an eight-hour flight, just because I'd asked them to?

Despite my early start to the planning in May, engaging an events team and investing $100,000 on the celebrations, I couldn't make up for my own crippling anxiety. I'm not proud to admit this, but I put key decisions off for so long that our own in-house events space was booked and we had to hold it elsewhere!

I have my events team leaders to thank for getting me on track despite all the tests I subjected their patience to. I only confirmed everything a few weeks before the date, and it took one of them yelling at me to get my own commitment in gear. Kudos to them both!

That was the turning point. Problems still came up, but the familiar, results-driven Marcus was back in gear. I made sure all 12 invitees showed up, and the President's Invite ended up being the company's most profitable event in a long time. The next year we scaled it up to 300 guests, but the first edition is still one of my fondest memories of my team's ability to work quickly under great stress and uncertainty, and take ownership of what happened.

What has this got to do with your role as a manager? It is the fact that, being closer to the ground than the key leaders of the company, you'll be the one managing the boss' expectations and supporting their role. Leaders need to empower their subordinates, but also build the relationship capital needed to work with their bosses. Your ability to do this could have great consequences for the whole company, and grows even more important the bigger the promises.

Instead, too many leaders surround themselves with yes-men who see riding their boss' coattails as their way to the top, and simply tell them what they want to hear. What I'm about to tell you could easily be mistaken for bootlicking or being a teacher's pet, but nothing could be further from the truth. It may have been true in the schoolyard, but we're all adults here and shouldn't be taking such attitudes into the workplace. Why is it so bad to help others get the results they need?

It's indeed true that an unpopular leader is not a strength for the team, but it's nothing short of counter-productive to let them (and yourself) fail, just to show them how poor their performance is.

Relationships and success

Think of the relationship between yourself and other deci-sion-makers and team members as a "bank". In the same way that you can only withdraw money you have previously deposited, your success communicating with them and getting them on your side needs you to have put in the work building up the relationship in the first place. The better it is, the more open you can be, the more seriously you will be taken, and the stronger your teamwork can be.

What are the best ways you can get the credibility needed to be listened to? The best is obviously performing well, and that means doing what's asked of you with as little fuss as possible. Do it even if you're not in full agreement, because what's happening here is that your bosses are trying their best to solve the problems entrusted to them. "With each of those problems," Willink points out, "I am the solution ... I am the person who can make things happen. And more importantly, I gain clout with the boss."[36]

At the beginning, my new superiors and I butted heads a lot, and some of my immediate subordinates were unhappy that I was in a seat they wanted. But when I spoke with one of the more antagonistic country heads reporting to me, I decided to throw us both an olive branch. "Okay, I'll leave you alone," I told him. "But here's our target, and if you think you can hit it without me, go ahead. If you can't and you need help, I'm available to provide it."

I knew full well that he wanted to make me look bad, and he was accusing me behind my back of plotting to fire the team to bring in my own people. Notice that I wasn't letting my ego or emotions dictate what happened, nor directly confronting the fact that we disagreed on so much. I had other options, including business in other Southeast Asian countries, all of which were booming; and I was giving him a face-saving way out of further disagreement.

If he wanted to keep doing things his way (and he was indeed doing well), he would have to compete with his colleagues and see who would come out on top. He agreed, and we moved on from that conversation.

He turned around when one of our resorts was holding a huge get-together for movers and shakers in Genting Highlands. Many of our business rivals would be there, and he needed my presence to help his team out. I was in Thailand at the time, and dropped everything there to join him. It turned out to be the right decision, and he ended the year with triple his assigned targets!

In effect, I'm doing for my own bosses and team members what I did for whales before — become the go-to person who can take care of the problems they face; or at least give them a listening ear. Former US Army General and Secretary of State Colin Powell put it like this:

Leadership is solving problems. The day the soldiers stop bringing you their problems is the day you stopped leading them. They have either lost confidence that you can help them or concluded that you do not care. Either case is a failure of leadership.

My reputation as a problem-solver is my best asset, and the most potent weapon I have in any partnership I must engage in, or any confrontation I must have with another person, no matter whether their position is higher or lower than me. That's more important than any personal disagreements I may have with them, or how they work. The only difference from my days starting out is that my team is there to help me build, refine and execute a plan.

That doesn't mean I limit myself to sales issues, because everything the customer experiences *is* a sales issue. Are service standards slipping? Let me see what I can do to encourage the wait staff, dealers, cooks and other team members to do better, and what resources I can allocate that will help.

Is the customer threatening to leave? I'll learn what he needs, and persuade him to come back. As we've seen, one of them was even on his way to my previous place of work, until I called and got him to return!

Are team members overpromising and leaving clients with a faulty impression of what we can provide? I'll sit down with them and see how their presentations and closes can be improved.

The glue of relationships

Take the time to know everyone around you; that is, your immediate bosses and subordinates. In the same way that we keep a record of every big customer, you need to under-stand each team mate's situation at home (as far as they're willing to share) and at work alike; their preferences and dis-likes, and their strengths and weaknesses. This isn't about manipulating them, but helping them get the best out of the talents and aptitudes they already have.

So take them out to coffee, talk about what things concern them inside and outside of work, and learn how to support your superiors and what obstacles to clear for your subordinates. Different people respond well to different approaches, so don't try to manage them with a one-size-fits-all attitude.

I'm where I am today because my managers saw I didn't work well being micromanaged, and set me free to use my abilities in their service. When I see similar "wild horses" among my team, I gently point them in the right direction and get out of their way; others need more time and guidance till they learn the ropes, but once they do it's off to the races. It's a matter of bringing out the best in everyone.

The more my team sees my interest in their careers, the better our relationship — even if we don't agree on every issue or otherwise don't get along. The more my bosses see how well we work together and solve problems (that is, the ones that matter to them), the more influence we have when it comes time to use it.

While a good leader should be open to (and indeed, welcome) any feedback or criticism, not everyone is like this. That's what makes the relationship capital you've built all the more important.

The idea here is to have open channels of communication up and down the chain of command. No one wants to see themselves as unheard and unrepresented, and this is true of both individuals and entire groups.

It is the opposite of putting a problem out of sight, out of mind. There should never be a fear of bringing bad news to the attention of those who need it. Communication problems tend to be what Harvard Business Review's Art Markman calls "the canary in the coal mine", or the first indication of a deeper, more systemic issue. "It's a signal that something is wrong, but it itself is probably not the problem."[37]

He gives a more specific example. The problem at one

organisation wasn't a lack of communication, but "that there was no clear structure defining what employees could and could not do". Vague job descriptions had worked when it was starting out, but as more employees came on, there was less opportunity to define their roles by observing others.

For good, usable information to come in, good communication and cooperation across teams and management levels is the baseline. Plans, guidelines and directives need to be simply and clearly stated, so that everyone understands their role and why it must be carried out. It has to be embedded in the culture of the whole company.

There's no need to wait for the C-suite to take action; meaningful change begins and ends with you. Here are some questions to ask yourself and your teammates:

1. Am I taking full ownership and responsibility for what happens, so that I'm in the best position to solve problems?

2. Are we problem-makers, or problem-solvers? What needs to be done to become more of the latter, and how will we know when we reach that status?

3. Who can I trust to give me the bad news, and correct our course if needed?

4. How is our relationship with our manager, and do we have a meaningful say in affairs beyond our own purview?

5. What can we do today that will build us into the team we want to be?

What we've learnt

1. Substance beats flash any day of the week, but what is ultimately needed is leadership that is confident enough to stay the course, yet humble enough to change when necessary.
2. Relationship is everything, for colleagues and customers alike. Build this relationship by performing well, being approachable for problems and getting to know them as people.
3. Bring out the best in your subordinates. They're the ones who'll be making the numbers for you, and there's no replacement for an open, trusting relationship with them.
4. Communicate goals, intent and plans simply and clearly up and down the chain of command, so leaders at all levels are empowered to plan and execute in line with the whole agenda.

Conclusion

There is no one-size-fits-all route to success. What we may perceive as the "answer" because a certain conventionally successful person did it is not necessarily accurate — it is rather our survivorship bias at play, committing a post hoc fallacy. And that's exactly what I'm *not* offering. By no means am I attempting to claim that my personal route to conventional success is a magical, foolproof one that works for everyone.

I believe that there is value in sharing a story like mine because it is unconventional. My riches weren't made by launching a successful tech startup; they were made attracting ultra high-net-worth individuals to casinos. I believe in the value of sharing a story like mine because it was challenging. As a poly dropout clueless about work-place politics and corporate culture, my arms were constantly twisted by work enemies fighting political wars I didn't even know existed, until I learnt the ropes and started outperforming them by leaps and bounds.

If you've made it this far, I think it is evident that the lessons I share in this book are not complex. They are simple things that may even feel obvious and simple common sense once repeated over a sustained period of time. Yet these are the very lessons that allowed me to succeed even as countless salespeople on various levels of seniority failed to do so, and I immensely wish someone had imparted them to me when I was oblivious and just starting out. In hindsight, these skills laid the groundwork for strong and close-knit relationships with important customers, some of whom went on to be good personal friends for life.

I hope that my personal experiences and the lessons learnt along the way have left you with something that will help, be it finding success in the same casino sales business or leaving a good impression on your interviewers at a university interview. At the very least, let this book be a testament to the fact that a disadvantaged start is no impenetrable fortress guarding success, and that underdog stories are real, happen close to you, and not limited to those that achieve academic success.

I wish you all the best on your own journey.

Closing Note
A Letter to My Son

This has been a very personal book, and my intention was to share the business lessons I've learnt along the way with anyone who's interested. That way, there's no more veil of secrecy when it comes to meeting and winning over the very rich; and more companies, hosts and salespeople can work with them to deliver incredible experiences all around.

It also represents my hope that a new generation will carry these principles forward, so that everyone will benefit. To that end, I've decided to close this book with a simple letter to my 10-year-old son. Here's what I would tell him, and anyone just starting out in working life:

Max,

As I write this, you are 10 and Dad is 42, and the COVID-19 pandemic is challenging all of us in new and unexpected ways.

This has been especially true for my sector, travel and hospitality. I left my job in June after much devotion and

sacrifice for a company and field that I love, and I'm sad-
dened by this turn of events; you can do everything right
and add incredible value, and still find yourself no longer
needed.

Of course, I got depressed and asked myself what more
could I have done. Was I underperforming? Hadn't I brought
my company to new heights? The numbers said more than
I could, and my superiors and I spent many hours discuss-
ing an alternate outcome. In the end, I simply accepted it,
congratulated them and wished them well.

It was certainly hard on all of us, but hard times are
what bring out the best in us. When you were still in Mummy's womb, I was still struggling to make ends meet — this
was when I ran Grandpa's wakeboarding business, a cake
delivery business and a weekend pet café. I was just doing
everything I could to bring in the dough for the family, and I
remember long nights wondering what to do whenever we
ran out of money. There wasn't even enough to buy the
ingredients we needed to make burgers to sell!

That situation then may have been more challenging,
but the solution was the same — to step up and take action.
I made up my mind to seek a day job that would start paying
bills and provide for the family, then pursue my passions
when I could.

I was chasing money, not something I loved. Never just
chase money, as it will only bring you sorrow and disappointment. I had spread myself too thin and dabbled in different things without identifying my true strengths. Besides
that, I trusted the wrong people and gave them money for

investments that were never fulfilled. Give people the benefit of the doubt, but always verify what they say, with professional help if needed!

The bottom line was that I couldn't focus on solving problems for our customers, something any successful business must do. With you on the way, it would've been a big mistake to stay in unproductive, meaningless business pursuits that I knew little about. I couldn't keep making mistakes, as I wanted to give you the best of everything I could afford.

I don't consider it a waste of time, though. Life has a weird but amazing way of making pieces of a puzzle fall into place.

In my pet café days, I got close to one of my mentors, Mr Lee. A very successful entrepreneur, he owned the pet farm we sourced our dogs from. He shared with me many lessons of life, and I'm still amazed at his success; he's self-educated, but he kept on learning and growing in one area that others valued — how to breed, bring up and sell dogs. He got so good at it that he is probably the number one "dog whisperer" in Singapore!

When he made his first pot of gold, he went on to learn other skills with the same focus and became even more successful. If there is one lesson that I learnt from him, it has been to focus on one thing at a time. What I did best was networking and selling, and so I focused on that out of pure necessity. I had nothing to fall back on.

This book would never have come about if not for you. I was very lucky at my down point to have been given an opportunity to join a big multi-national resort company, and although my time there was short, it laid strong foundations for my career. It let me devote everything to learning the hospitality and gaming trade as best I could.

I've spent the last 10 years challenging the industry and myself on how we can enhance every aspect of it, not just the small slice we're directly responsible for. How could we uplift customer experiences and ensure they kept coming back? How could we find the best talents, to sell the dream to clients and team members alike?

No one does this perfectly, and my own direct approach, I freely admit, has its strengths and weaknesses. I make no apologies for it, but looking back, could more collaboration have led to more success? Probably, and there are certainly customers who've been reached in other ways.

The point is to be yourself and work with others as a team. Authenticity is a rare thing, so use whatever approach you deem fit as long as what is intended is achieved. Everyone should hone their own style to the end of being part of a great team and solving problems. I am sure you will do well in this aspect, as you've got great charm and charisma. Remember, respect can only be earned, not commanded — and I hope you will earn the respect of everyone you meet and work with.

Until the pandemic, I had an amazing journey in this industry — but it came at the price of missing so many of your growing-up years. It's one of my biggest regrets, and I'm truly sorry for that; I swear I'll do what it takes to make up for it. In a way, I'm thankful how the pandemic slowed everything down, and gave us the opportunity we needed to spend so much fun time together. We're certainly closer than before, and I'm glad to finally hold your hand when we go out. You've given me new-found strength, and taught me the value of family all over again.

With so much affected, we're all uncertain what the immediate future holds. This book sums up my journey so far and what I've learnt, and I'm confident these principles will remain true no matter what happens. It's my play-book, and I hope it'll help others as I prepare for my next adventure!

Before I sign off, I want to leave you with a life lesson from Mr Lee:

First, things are toughest at the beginning. Earning your first $1 million is the hardest, because you must do it on your own; you need to work very hard and save as much as you can. Luxury items will need to wait.

Second, once you do this, you can collaborate much better with others. Do this with either your closest friends or business acquaintances. Again, I want to stress the need for due diligence and the help of independent professionals. There are fees to be paid but I can assure you, what you spend is negligible in the bigger scheme of things. Due diligence and trusting your friends are separate entities, and if your "friends" are resisting that, there is probably something wrong with the project.

Your team will have to pool all their resources together, and there will be more work than what you put in for your first million — but there'll now be people to work, push through and share your frustration with. As before, luxury can wait.

At the third stage, get serious professional help. This will be when you have $5 million or so, and private bankers will knock on your doors. Use them, and use their transparency in the process to get the best you can afford. Have your lawyers vet every proposal to set up your portfolio, so you enjoy both constant passive income and capital gains. Now is the time for responsibly enjoying luxuries — you've earned them!

That said, whichever stage you're at, enjoy your life as you only live once. Learn to take good care of yourself, as Daddy and Mummy won't be here forever, as much as we want to be. I have all confidence in you that you will make your own mark one day.

Remember, having lots of money does not necessarily mean you are happy. Don't chase it; find a way to do what you love in a way that other people love and value too, and I know that will lead you to true riches.

I love you, Max.

Your Daddy

Appendix
What We've Learnt

1 One Odd Start

1. Be observant of how others behave, particularly the better off. Pay special attention to how they dress and what they talk about.
2. Sales to high-net-worth customers and regular people have roughly the same approach — listening to them, understanding their needs and building a relationship, before any products come into the picture.
3. The skills in this book don't just apply to the casino trade, but can be used to build strong relationships with high-net-worth customers in any area.

2 Casinos: Losing, Winning and So Much More

1. Gambling isn't simply a vice. Thanks to integrated resorts, it's an experience you can sell alongside tours, hotel stays, theatre shows and many other attractive activities.

2. If you yourself must gamble, do it right and keep your greed in check. Your primary role is to help your customers get the best possible experience.
3. Being a salesperson means giving up safety and stability for an unpredictable, round-the-clock experience that brings both increased risk and greater rewards. It's certainly not for everyone.
4. Be prepared to build the relationship by the means available to you — even if you must be ready to help clients out at odd hours.

3 The Foundations of Salescraft

1. As a salesperson, your aim is to close better deals faster.
2. Sales is a team effort and needs good co-operation and strategy. Everything you do should be part of an overall plan.
3. Your role is to work with the customer to create an experience that they will enjoy, and that the company can provide.
4. Learn the role that is best suited for your personality, and the best way you can build good relationships with the customers you serve.
5. Play the long game, and keep learning and growing. Don't be discouraged — over time, the closure process will become easier and easier.

4 **Hunters and Gatherers**

1. A sales team needs both Hunters and Gatherers. Each role needs a different personality type, so you need to know which one you can be.
2. Surprises can happen. We simulate them in interviews, so prepare accordingly by understanding how to deal with them. Remember, put people above possessions, and de-escalate conflicts quickly.
3. A sales role *requires* you to actively tend to your relationships with customers, so that you can form close friendships and gain their trust.
4. Each sales meeting needs you to be fully alert and on your toes. Keep the company's needs in mind, and be careful what you commit to. It's not what's in your head, but what's in your bones.

5 **Whales: A Field Guide**

1. Approach sales from the customer's point of view, not your own. What's important is what matters to *him*, not you.
2. Understand the different types of whales. Generally, earners seek risk and thrill, while inheritors want a good time with plenty of fun.
3. Meet whales and get to know them via informal events that give them something they want.
4. Start by building relationships, finding common ground and learning more about each prospect. The

sale only enters the picture *after* a strong friendship has been built.

6 Selling the Dream — Quickly and Often

1. We don't sell a company; we sell an experience that customers want.
2. Focus on knowing them as people and becoming their friends, before drawing out their needs. Avoid talking too much about yourself or your needs until the relationship is strong enough.
3. Work alongside your bosses. Understand their duties and who they report to, so you become an asset to them.
4. Build team loyalty through setting a good example yourself, and appreciating everyone's hard work.

7 The Right Impression

1. Make an unforgettable impression. The more such experiences created at your meetings, the better.
2. Pay attention to every detail, and do work you can be rightly proud of.
3. Accentuate the positive and create favourable impressions. This is being clear about features and benefits, not being dishonest.
4. Genuine care for others cannot be faked. It must be real, and come through at the first meeting, the last and every one in between.

8 Do Your Homework

1. Know your product, and anticipate any questions that might arise. If necessary, role-play them with a friend.
2. Front-load the work through as much research as possible on the client himself, and your understanding of the groups that he or she is a member of. Use this knowledge to plan the discussion accordingly, so you're never stuck.
3. Use media, both traditional and social, as a research tool. There is no such thing as too much information.

9 Platform Marketing and Social Media

1. Social media can be an asset or a liability. Use it wisely, and remember it is not a replacement for deep in-person conversation.
2. Many thought leaders blog, or use Twitter. Check them out, and keep abreast of industry developments.
3. Tailor your use of social media platforms to your company, industry and objectives. Keep things professional, and when in doubt, don't post it.

10 The Three-Meeting Rule

1. Sales meetings should be held with an eye on the relationship, your own resources within the company and your own professional conduct.

2. Use the three-meeting rule as an initial guide. Plan out what needs to be accomplished at the end of each meeting, so you can quickly decide whether to keep prospecting them or move on.

3. Meetings are a chance to learn more about what your customer truly wants, and what drives them. Come up with a reward, then plan out together how both of you can make their dream come true.

4. There can be deal sales, and relationship sales. All sales should be a good deal, but a strong relationship can often drive the sale all by itself.

11 When Things Change, So Do You

1. No approach — not even my own three-meeting rule — is set in stone. Every interaction is different, so prepare well *and* be ready to adapt your script and plans.

2. Work with confidence and pride in yourself and your services. You're building a relationship and offering something they want, so act like it!

3. Understand that money and price are simply small parts of the package. If you differentiate well and offer something your customer truly wants, price matters very little.

4. Solve problems by pre-emptively building a good reputation, taking responsibility, admitting your mistakes and working to find solutions.

12 **A Whole New World**

1. Commit to keeping your wits about you. Staying aware and understanding the consequences of your promises is hard enough when you're sober.
2. Follow all company directives regarding vice, and don't become addicted yourself.
3. If you cannot drink or accept the client's hospitality, graciously decline by pointing to your responsibilities towards him, your health or your loved ones.

13 **Focus on Yourself**

1. Invest in yourself and look for new challenges to grow your skills and value.
2. See less-than-satisfactory leaders as an opportunity, not an obstacle.
3. Take ownership of everything that happens with your team, while guiding and empowering them to solve problems without you.
4. Treat others the way you want to be treated, and go the extra mile for them.
5. Crises don't create faults; they reveal them.

14 **Service Recovery or Bust!**

1. Service recovery must be part of a constant process of customer engagement and drawing out, listening to and acting on feedback.

2. Empower team members to deal with problems immediately as needed, so only what is escalated to you needs to be personally dealt with.
3. Be grateful for the feedback and don't get defensive. The relationship is more important than your ego.
4. Be on the lookout for systemic issues, so you can resolve them before they become more serious problems and begin driving guests away.

15 Everyone Is Needed

1. Get the right people, and get them on board with your plans and purposes. No one is above learning from their subordinates.
2. Empower subordinates to make their own plans and take action — within the limits set by higher management and in line with their goals.
3. Be open to change, and adapt your plans as needed. COVID-19 will not be the last major shock to your industry, and the lessons you learn here must be carried forward.
4. Leaders need to trust each other, and a well-run team will have clear areas of responsibility in line with everyone's strengths and weaknesses.

16 Managing Your Bosses

1. Substance beats flash any day of the week, but what is ultimately needed is leadership that is confident

enough to stay the course, yet humble enough to change when necessary.

2. Relationship is everything, for colleagues and customers alike. Build this relationship by performing well, being approachable for problems and getting to know them as people.

3. Bring out the best in your subordinates. They're the ones who'll be making the numbers for you, and there's no replacement for an open, trusting relationship with them.

4. Communicate goals, intent and plans simply and clearly up and down the chain of command, so leaders at all levels are empowered to plan and execute in line with the whole agenda.

Notes

1. "MM Lee on Casino", *The Singapore Commentator*, 3 December 2004, at http://sg-comment.blogspot.sg/2004/12/mm-lee-on-casino.html.

2. "A Brief History of Casino Resorts", *Travel with a Mate*, at http://www.travelwithamate.com/history-of-casino-resorts.

3. True to its integrated resort design, its centrepiece is a hotel with over 2,000 rooms, topped with a skypark and its famous infinity pool. Below it, there are gourmet restaurants, luxury shops, a museum, a theatre and an ice-skating rink. The casino itself only takes up a small part of the total floor area.

4. For an explanation of the Pareto principle, see Kalid Azad, "Understanding the Pareto Principle (the 80/20 Rule), Better Explained", at http://betterexplained.com/articles/understanding-the-pareto-principle-the-8020-rule.

5. Quoted in Michael Kaplan, "Confessions of the Man Who Wins Big When You Lose It All", *Thrillist*, 6 August 2015, at https://www.thrillist.com/entertainment/nation/confessions-of-the-man-who-wins-big-when-you-lose-it-all-in-vegas.

6. Jamie Fortier, "Picking a Hunter or Gatherer: The Ultimate Hiring Decision", *McHenry Consulting*, 3 January 2013, at http://www.mchenryconsulting.net/content/picking-hunter-or-gatherer-ultimate-hiring-decision.

7. Dale Carnegie, *How to Enjoy Your Life and Your Job* (New York, NY: Pocket Books, 1986), p. 112.

8. Ibid.

9. Ramit Sethi, "Why Won't Anyone Be Honest with You?" *I Will Teach You to Be Rich*, at http://www.iwillteachyoutoberich. com/blog/why-wont-anyone-be-honest-with-you.

10. Quoted in Paul Sullivan, *The Thin Green Line: Money Secrets of the Super Wealthy* (New York, NY: Simon & Schuster, 2015), Prologue.

11. Ibid.

12. P&L stands for Profit and Loss, an indicator of a company's performance that is reported in a statement to investors.

13. Lawrence A Cunningham, "The Philosophy of Warren E. Buffett", *The New York Times*, 1 May 2015, at http://www.nytimes.com/ 2015/05/02/business/dealbook/the-philosophy-of-warren-e-buffett.html?_r=0.

14. Ibid.

15. Joyce Lim, "Overnight millionaire: Record penthouse deal nets 26-year-old property agent $1.5m", *The Straits Times*, 29 May 2015, at http://www.straitstimes.com/singapore/overnight-millionaire-record-penthouse-deal-nets-26-year-old-property-agent-15m.

16. An excellent reference on introverted people and how to tap their talent is Susan Cain's *Quiet: The Power of Introverts in a World that Can't Stop Talking* (New York, NY: Random House, 2012). It's very likely that an introverted whale will have read it, or will respond well to the ideas in it.

17. Deke Castleman, *Whale Hunt in the Desert: Secrets of a Vegas Superhost* (Las Vegas, NV: Huntington Press Publishing, 2008), p. 2.

18. Ramit Sethi, "Why Won't Anyone Be Honest with You?", *I Will Teach You to Be Rich*, at http://www.iwillteachyoutoberich. com/blog/why-wont-anyone-be-honest-with-you.

19. Neil Strauss, *The Game* (New York, NY: HarperCollins, 2009).

20. Ibid.

21. "DISC FAQ", Discreports.com, (no date), at http://www. discreports.com/ed-center/faq.

22. Ramit Sethi, "3 Essential Systems for Starting an Online Business", *I Will Teach You to Be Rich*, at http://www.iwillteach youtoberich.com/blog/3-essential-systems-for-starting-an-online-business.

23. Dominique Mosbergen, "Single Mom Fired From Daycare Center For Facebook Post Saying She Hates 'Being Around A Lot Of Kids'", *The Huffington Post*, 5 May 2015, at http://www.huffingtonpost.com/2015/05/05/daycare-worker-fired-facebook-kaitlyn-walls_n_7210122.html.

24. For examples, see Alex Bracetti, "25 Facebook Posts That Have Gotten People Fired", *Complex*, 11 May 2012, at http://www.complex.com/pop-culture/2012/05/25-facebook-posts-that-have-gotten-people-fired.

25. Nick Vujicic, "Stand Strong USA: Photos", Facebook, 9 December 2015.

26. Interviewed in A Warrior's Journey (2000). "Bruce Lee", Wikiquote, at https://en.wikiquote.org/wiki/Bruce_Lee#Quotes.

27. Jocko Willink and Leif Babin, *Extreme Ownership: How U.S. Navy SEALs Lead and Win* (New York, NY: St Martin's Press, 2017), "Jocko Podcast Questions and Answers."

28. Kouzes, Posner and Calvert, *Stop Selling and Start Leading: How to Make Extraordinary Sales Happen* (Hoboken, NJ: John Wiley & Sons, 2018), p. 146.

29. Ross Cranwell, "Service Recovery: How to Win Customers Back After a Negative Experience," *Stella Connect*, 25 September 2019, at https://stellaconnect.com/2019/09/25/win-customers-back-with-service-recovery.

30. "The Power of Empowerment," The Ritz-Carlton Leadership Center, 19 March 2019, at https://ritzcarltonleadershipcenter.com/2019/03/19/the-power-of-empowerment.

31. Willink and Babin, *Extreme Ownership*.

32. Ibid.

33. Jocko Willink, *Leadership Strategy and Tactics* (New York, NY: St Martin's Press, 2019), "Core Tenets".

NOTES

34. Steven Pressfield, *The Profession* (New York, NY: Crown Publishing, 2011), "1: A Brother".

35. Willink, *Leadership Strategy and Tactics,* "Laws of Combat and Principles of Leadership".

36. Ibid.

37. Art Markman, "'Poor Communication' Is Often a Symptom of a Different Problem", *Harvard Business Review*, 22 February 2017, at https://hbr.org/2017/02/poor-communication-is-often-a-symptom-of-a-different-problem.

Acknowledgements

I would like to thank my family and loved ones, for tolerating my nonsensical mood swings and big dreams.

Many thanks to my godmother, who opened up a whole new world and offered me an experience that no child from a poor family could have had.

To John Chong, who gave me a chance to get into this business.

To everyone who still believes in me, I will try my best not to let you down. To all my clients that I have served (or have yet to serve), I am nothing without your support and guidance. Everything I am today is because of you.

To the readers of this book, congratulations on taking this step in investing in yourself! I hope you enjoyed reading this book as much as I did writing it.

To those who still have nothing good to say about me: Thanks for all your unwitting encouragement! I won't be a hypocrite and wish you well, but I can hope I've helped give your competitors the edge they need.

About the Author

Marcus Lim has spent over a decade as a host and marketer at several of the largest casino and resort chains in the world, rising to the position of President of International Marketing in the Star Entertainment Group. He has successfully marketed gaming resorts and first-class entertainment to a clientele worth billions of dollars.

An entrepreneur at heart, Marcus has headed his own companies in defence, business consultation and sea sports. He holds an MBA from Singapore Management University.

About the Co-Author

Pearlin Siow runs Boss of Me, a boutique book-writing agency that specialises in helping people write as well as publish books. Together with her team of content specialists, Pearlin has produced several bestselling biographies for top entrepreneurs and companies in Singapore. The agency's clients range from billionaires to stay-at-home mothers.